Emotional Intelligence

In A Week

Jill Dann

The Teach Yourself series has been trusted around the world
for over 60 years. This new series of 'In A Week' business books
is designed to help people at all levels and around the world to
further their careers. Learn in a week, what the experts learn in
a lifetime.

Jill Dann works on practical issues as a coach and facilitator with board and MD leadership teams on clarification of their strategy. Identifying and resolving root cause issues using her coaching capability and insight, Jill works one-to-one and with groups leading significant transformations, mergers and acquisitions. She has worked in the USA, Australia, New Zealand and Europe.

Acknowledgements

I would like to recognise the following people:

My husband Derek G Dann has continued to encourage me to write and to provide excellent proofreading and feedback capability. I look forward to publishing a Hodder Emotional Intelligence Workbook with him in 2012.

Barbara Murray provided great practitioner insights at the proof stage and useful text or references.

Dr Sherria Hoskins, Head of Psychology at the University of Portsmouth, who when I asked her about the current thinking on self-awareness introduced me to Dr Clare Wilson, Director of the Quality of Life, Health and Wellbeing Research Group, who provided very useful resources on mindfulness.

Dr Cathie Palmer-Woodward BA (Hons) BPhil MA – the Friday chapter mindmaps were developed originally with Cathie while working together on a learning organization agenda for the launch of two banks: egg and if.com. Cathie continues to be a powerhouse of creative thinking in consulting and coaching.

Sandie Pinches, Master Coach and Managing Director of Above & Beyond Coaching, has continued to be a great source of encouragement and positive affirmation.

Emotional Intelligence

Jill Dann

www.inaweek.co.uk

Hodder Education

338 Euston Road, London NW1 3BH.

Hodder Education is an Hachette UK company

First published in UK 2001 by Hodder Education

First published in US 2012 by The McGraw-Hill Companies, Inc.

This edition published 2012

Previous editions of this book were published by Hodder in 2001, 2002

www.hoddereducation.co.uk

Typeset by Cenveo Publisher Services.

Printed and bound by CPI Group (UK) Ltd, Croydon, CR0 4YY.

Contents

Introduction

Emotional Intelligence (EI) has emerged as a potential concept for explaining variance in behaviour not accounted for by traditional measures of personality traits or general academic intelligence (traditionally called IQ). The book has been written to enable aspiring and junior managers to gain confidence in the main areas that EI touches in everyday life, in business life and equally to those in the public or voluntary sectors. Taken one day at a time, the chapter content builds on that of previous days and the structure comprises:

Sunday: Learn how emotional intelligence is relevant to you and how and why there are benefits to developing higher levels.

Monday: Learn how heightened your self-awareness is and the implications on your life currently, for your personal life and as a leader of others.

Tuesday: Learn about the mechanisms of self-control, emotional memory and consciousness to take control of behavioural patterns.

Wednesday: Learn about stress identification and beneficial management strategies.

Thursday: Diagnose and explore change in your organization to create change, manage uncertainty and gain momentum.

Friday: Design and create a new emotionally literate culture, learning environment and a coaching ethos.

Saturday: Learn how to design and tailor successful personal development.

Using the guidance, the end of this book marks the *beginning* of your personal development programme tailored *by* you specifically *for* you. You can monitor yourself developing and applying emotional and social competencies.

More than you may think, there are many additional sources of insight, transferable knowledge and wisdom – written and online, the local community, friends and family, formal and informal groups, education or training.

Development milestones

In the last chapter, Saturday, you are assisted in methods to establish development milestones stretching out into the future. It is worth understanding that *in childhood* there are four basic categories of developmental milestones:

- **Physical milestones** involve both large and fine motor skills. The first to develop are usually the large-motor skills such as sitting up, standing, crawling and walking. Fine-motor skills involve precise movements such as grasping a spoon, holding a crayon, drawing shapes and picking up small objects.
- **Cognitive milestones** refer to a child's ability to think, to learn and to solve problems. Examples are: an infant learning how to respond appropriately to facial expressions and a child at nursery school learning the alphabet.
- **Social and emotional milestones** are centred on children gaining a better understanding of their own emotions and the emotions of others. These milestones also involve learning how to interact and play with other people.
- **Communication milestones** involve both language and nonverbal communication. A one-year-old learning how to say his first words and a five-year-old learning some of the basic rules of grammar are examples of important communication milestones.

The content of the early chapters will encourage you to explore and reflect on your development to date, to consider your current support structure and to engage with your inner self so that you emerge with more self-knowledge and self-motivation.

Overview of EI

Experts are beginning to agree that types of intelligence other than IQ (Intelligence Quotient) have evolved as *human capacities* over the last two million years. Low Emotional Intelligence Quotient or EQ can be perceived as the absence of control over the outcome of a situation. Do you ever feel like this is the case – you keep getting 'poor luck' or cannot influence better results? Therefore, when you have a high EQ you are adept at interpreting the emotional roots of your thinking and behaviours and *choosing* your actions for beneficial outcomes. You may also be capable of making good insights into the behaviours and reactions of others through empathy and rapport.

These topics are explored, step by step. You are going to gain an understanding through finding out about:

Pessimism or optimism

A milestone history of EI-related concepts

Measurement of EQ – a list of assessments

Identifying the benefits of 'emotional fitness'

How EI is learnable

When you get emotionally hijacked

How will it change me?

How and why to keep a journal

The following background sections are intended to give you opportunities to explore other EI-related concepts plus more insight on directing your own development through raised self-awareness and self-control.

SUNDAY

MONDAY

TUESDAY

WEDNESDAY

THURSDAY

FRIDAY

SATURDAY

Pessimism or optimism

You may have encountered individuals who have different attributes in how they explain to themselves why they experience a particular event in either a positive or a negative fashion. Psychologists label this 'explanatory style' and have identified three components:

- **Personal:** This component involves how one explains where the cause of an event arises. People experiencing events may see themselves as the cause; that is, they have internalized the cause for the event. For example: 'I always forget to make that turning' (i.e. internal) as opposed to, 'That left turn sneaks up on you' (i.e. external).
- **Permanent:** This component involves how one explains the *extent* of the cause. People may see the situation as unchangeable. For example: 'I *always* lose my car keys' or 'I *never* forget a face'.
- **Pervasive:** This component involves how one explains the extent of the *effects*. People may see the situation as affecting all aspects of their life. For example: 'I can't do anything right' or 'Everything I touch seems to turn to gold'.

Individuals who generally blame themselves for negative events tend to believe that such events will continue indefinitely. They let such events affect many aspects of their lives displaying what is called a *pessimistic explanatory style*. A person's explanatory style is believed to influence their view of the future and, as a result, their projected perceptions and subsequent behaviour. If a pleasing event is experienced an optimist would exhibit an *internal, stable and global explanatory style*, whereas a pessimist would be showing *external, unstable and specific explanatory style*.

The concept of explanatory style encompasses a wide range of possible responses to both positive and negative occurrences (shades of grey), rather than solely a black or white difference between optimism and pessimism. Significantly, an individual does not necessarily show a uniform explanatory style in all aspects of life, but may exhibit varying responses to different types of events.

The prospect of identifying when, where and why you have a particular explanatory style is one example of *self-awareness*. Reflecting on any variation of explanatory style is *self-observation*.

Choosing to be more optimistic is an example of *self-control*. These are the topics, covered in this and the following two chapters, which are utilized subsequently throughout the book and beyond into the period covered by your Personal Development Plan.

There are case studies where *'learned optimism'* has had startlingly good results on the morale and performance of sales teams. L'Oreal ran an emotional intelligence programme which started to select sales agents on the basis of their emotional competencies. In the first year of implementation, these sales agents outsold by $91,370 their counterparts who were not selected on this basis. This outcome of the EI programme led to a net in-year increase to L'Oreal of $2,558,360. Those selected on the basis of emotional competencies also had a 63 per cent lower turnover during the first year than those selected in the typical way (which in turn saves money on replacing people, recruitment, advertising and HR processes).

A milestone history of EI-related concepts

EI is not new and there have been many related concepts over the last 150–200 years. In the last 20 years, there has been more science available about the brain and the ability to map the activity of specific areas of the brain as it occurs. Some leaps forward have occurred as a result of the study of individuals with damaged areas of the brain, where the impact of the absence of a capacity can be discerned. Patients with moderate or severe traumatic brain injury (TBI) may show impairment in decision-making processes such as in making personal moral decisions: those involving strong emotions and survival or those that require a cost-benefit analysis (i.e. selecting an action which leads to an outcome that has 'greater good'). In other cases, the results have been obtained through counselling practice and the development of techniques to develop well-being and avoid or overcome mental illness.

Some interesting results came out of the (blind) study of brain scans of a mixture of individuals which split out with 100 per cent accuracy, those individuals known to be psychopaths (in custody at the time). They displayed a lack of capacity in several brain centres dealing with emotions and the processing of sensory inputs; the very 'muscles' humans want to exercise to improve and become more adept at managing themselves and others. The following is a selection of milestones for which there are ample resources available online, in other books and research papers.

Year	Originator	EI related concept
1859	Darwin	the importance of emotional expression for survival and adaptation
1920	E.L. Thorndike	'social intelligence' distinct from abstract or academic intelligence
1935	Doll	'social competence'
1940	Wechsler	'nonintellective intelligence'
1948	Leeper	'emotional thought'
1966	Leuner	'emotional intelligence'
1967	Seligman/Maier	'learned helplessness'
1973	Sifneos	'alexithymia' (cognitive-affective deficits)
1980	Howard Gardner	'multiple intelligences': linguistic, logical-mathematical, musical, bodily-kinaesthetic, spatial-visual, interpersonal (other people's feelings), intrapersonal (self-awareness), naturalistic, spiritual/existential, and moral.
1983	Gardner	'personal intelligences'
1983	Sternberg	'practical intelligences'
1985	Bagby & Taylor	Twenty-item Toronto Alexithymia Scale (TAS-20) Scale)
1985	Bar-On	'Emotional Quotient (EQ)' assessing emotional and social functioning
1989	Saarni	'emotional competency'
1990	Mayer & Salovey	'emotional intelligence': brain function and cognitive ability
1995	Goleman	'emotional intelligence' - popularized the term
1996	Dulewicz & Higgs	'IQ, EQ and MQ'
1998	Joseph LeDoux	Discovery of the emotional brain's ability to be one jump ahead of the neo-cortex
2000	Mayer & Cobb	'EI' - the ability to process emotional information, particularly as it involves the perception, assimilation, understanding, and management of emotion.

Year	Originator	EI related concept
2005	Boyatzis/McKee	'resonant leadership' – mindfulness, hope and compassion producing resilient leaders with resonance of heart, mind, body and spirit
2006	Joseph Forgas	'affect infusion' – explaining how mild feeling shifts influence memory recall, judgement and behaviour
2006	Goleman/Boyatzis	The Emotional and Social Competence Inventory (ESCI) –pilot measured 12 competencies
2006/7	Goleman	'social intelligence' – the brain is designed to be social; we are wired to connect, to use the neural bridge to link up when we engage with another person, to be 'contagious' emotionally
2008/9	Karl Albrecht	Social intelligence such as applied to customer value management – various works
2009	Paul Gilbert	the compassionate mind – overcoming negative self-talk, the neuroscience of affection and the importance of affection in our lives
2009	The International Positive Psychology Association (IPPA)	positive psychology – a holistic and compassionate approach to psychology focussing on mental well-being instead of a focus on mental illness. The 1st World Congress took place in Philadelphia.
2011	Professor Martin Seligman	flourish – building on his texts about learned helplessness, learned optimism, and documenting ten years of 'research' and the application of positive psychology (the focus is on wellness – not mental illness)

The first use of the term *Emotional Intelligence* (EI) appeared in the German publication *Praxis der Kinderpsychologie und Kinderpsychiatrie* by Leuner in 1966. In it, Leuner discusses women who reject their social roles due to them being separated at an early age from their mothers. He suggested that they had a low 'Emotional Intelligence' (EI) and prescribed LSD for their treatment (after all, this was the 1960s).

However, EI first appeared in English in a doctoral dissertation by Payne in 1986 ('A study of emotion: developing emotional intelligence, self-integration, relating to fear, pain, and desire'). He advocated fostering EI in schools by liberating emotional experience through therapy.

In the early 1990s, Jack Mayer, Peter Salovey, David Caruso and a few others began some serious research into EI as a human capacity or brain function. However, it was Daniel Goleman who popularized the term in the late 1990s when he came across their research while working as a science writer for the *New York Times* and he wrote some books on the subject.

Revelle (1995) wrote that there are three aspects of human nature:

● How all people are alike
● How some people are alike
● How all people are unique

Thus EI becomes:

● a general quality of human beings possessed by every normal person
● a quantitative spectrum of individual differences in which they can be ranked or ordered
● a qualitative, fine-grained account in which there are no comparisons between people.

EI nowadays seems to be mostly concerned with the second option above – ranking people on some type of emotional scale. This is perhaps because of the term itself. Intelligence is hard to define, but the means by which we come to understand it is through various measurements of individual human capacity.

Measurement of EQ – a list of assessments

A number of different EI assessments or 'tests' have been developed. The core proposition is similar; you can develop better self-awareness, self-regulation and the ability to use your senses to enhance your health, success in relationships or to influence others. Assessment gives individuals information about their own competence either through self-scoring or through 360-degree instruments (reverse appraisal of managers, using feedback from peers as well as seniors).

The following table is a summary of the main EI schools of thought and the most widely used and trademarked assessment tools.

Assessment tool	Description
EIQ™ (Dulewicz & Higgs)	Developed in 1999 at Henley Management College in the UK, Higgs is now at Southampton University. The Emotional Intelligence Questionnaire offers both self-report and 360-degree questionnaires, with the latter enabling an all-round assessment of an individual's performance from peers, colleagues and managers.
Multifactor Emotional Intelligence Scale®MEIS	The MEIS is a test of ability rather than a self-report measure. The test-taker performs a series of tasks that are designed to assess the person's ability to perceive, identify, understand, and work with emotion. There is very little for predictive validity in work situations.
MSCEIT® 'Mayer, Salovey, Caruso Emotional Intelligence Test'	The only ability measure of EQ, the MSCEIT requires you to actually use your abilities in taking the test with questions where you look at faces, for example, and identify what emotions are present. It helps you understand the actual intelligence behind emotions: perceiving, using, understanding, and managing feelings.
SEI™, Six Seconds Emotional Intelligence Test	Focussed on self-development, SEI is based on the Six Seconds' EQ-in-action model: Know Yourself, Choose Yourself, Give Yourself. The test measures eight fundamental skills in these three areas. Report comes with over 20 pages of interpretation and development suggestions.
OVS, Organizational Vital Signs™ by Six Seconds	Organizational Vital Signs is an organizational climate assessment that gives a clear picture of how people are relating to each other and the workplace. Unlike the other tests, OVS is designed to assess a group or an organization to show the context in which individuals perform. The test measures six factors: Trust, Collaboration, Accountability, Leadership, Alignment, Adaptability. These factors statistically predict over 50 per cent of productivity + customer service + retention.
EQ Map® by Essi Systems	With a much broader perspective, the EQ Map helps people put emotional intelligence into a workplace context. The Map is self-scored, so you can do it completely on your own; it has questions along the lines of, 'How well do you recognize emotions in people?' The 14 main scales include emotional awareness, emotional expression, resilience, outlook, trust, and personal power. It also has four outcome scales to show the benefit of increasing the first 14. The EQ Map includes an interpretation guide booklet.

Assessment tool	Description
EQ-i® by Reuven Baron	This self-report instrument was designed to assess those personal qualities that enabled some people to possess better 'emotional well-being' than others. The EQ-i® has been used to assess thousands of individuals, and its reliability and validity is well documented. Less is known about its predictive validity in work situations.
Emotional Intelligence Appraisal® by Talent Smart	There are three versions of this test. All use the Daniel Goleman 4-quadrant model: Self-awareness, Other-awareness, Self-management, Relationship-management. All take about seven minutes to complete, and all come with six months of e-learning and a valuable goal-tracking reminder system.
ECI® (Emotional Competence Inventory) by Hay Group	The ECI is a 360-degree appraisal tool where people who know the individual rate him or her on 20 competencies that are believed to be linked to emotional intelligence.
ESCI™ Emotional & Social Competence Inventory by Hay Group	Piloted in 2006, the 2010 ESCI Hay Group data shows (from 4,322 participants) that those who have high emotional self-awareness often or consistently display 9 ESCI competencies at strength. Conversely, those who never or sometimes display it show less than one competency at strength often or consistently. This leads to an assertion that emotional self-awareness or emotional literacy are at the heart of EI. It also calls into question the relationship with leadership styles; those with 10 or more ESCI strengths show a wide range of leadership styles, which can be utilized appropriately with changing organizational needs and the needs of the team members. In sharp contrast, those with low self-awareness create a negative organizational climate, which fails to motivate employees.

If you accept that emotional intelligence can be measured, then the next question is 'Can emotional intelligence be developed?' My recommendation is that the reader should focus on development and not become hooked on measurement alone. However, it is useful to have an assessment at the start of an EI development period and one about a year into it.

To determine why EI is important and should be a development priority, you need to look at the personal case for doing so. EI is backed up by a great deal of data and research as can be found by following up the details in each of the tables in this chapter (milestones and assessments).

Indentifying the benefits of 'emotional fitness'

Over the last 30 years, many people have tackled their physical fitness and taken charge of their diet to establish a good life balance. People who go to fitness centres, gyms and health spas are generally goal-oriented and want to be more effective.

Many people stop exercising because they 'lose motivation'. Having to spend 30–40 minutes practising relaxation techniques to wind down at the end of a busy day is very time-consuming. If this is on top of a beauty regime and the gym three or four times a week, it is even more protracted. However, if you are constantly looking after your emotional fitness, it is unnecessary to have to recover from turmoil at work and in your personal life.

The benefits to you of implementing the EI development in this book can be:

- improving your interpersonal skills and relationship success by acquiring knowledge, insight and increasing your self-awareness
- gaining an understanding of how to reduce the 'after the event' effort to relax as well as support stress management strategies that reduce the likelihood of long-term illness
- becoming equipped with basic skills to deconstruct your own behaviour in areas where it is mystifying or unhelpful, and to generate foresight rather than hindsight about your behaviour
- gaining an understanding of those factors that contribute to your emotional well-being.

Through a combination of the above, you can generate a new way of being in the 21st century and save yourself some time.

How EI is learnable

Raising EQ is possible because EI is learnable. Modern neuroscience tells us that the emotional centre of the brain learns differently to the cognitive centre. You can learn to fine tune or to increase your use of different parts of the human brain. Emotional memories and memories about emotions are processed differently by the brain, which we will look at in Tuesday's chapter.

As you go through the exercises suggested in this book, it will occur to you how suitable they feel for how you learn best. Which ways of learning do you find most helpful? If you do not know how to explore your learning preferences, I suggest that you do some research. As originally described by David Kolb, in his 1984 *Experiential Learning* (Prentice-Hall), your preferred learning style may be to:

● engage in immediate activity rather than pausing to reflect on what can be concluded
● envision the problem and to develop a set of options
● think through the practical implementation of solutions.

Remember what it was like when you first learned to drive a car? You did not know what you did not know.

Do you remember the way that you were treated by the instructor and how it affected your ability to retain the lessons and to maintain your self-confidence?

The Learning Ladder

Learning Ladder Rung	What it feels like when you are on it	EQ Competencies
4. Unconscious competence	You feel as if you have always known this or been proficient in this skill	Awareness of feelings Personal insight
3. Conscious competence	You know what you know and feel clumsy practising this new-found knowledge or skill	Self-assurance Self-regulation Authenticity
2. Conscious incompetence	You now know what you do not know and you may not like it	Accountability Flexibility Self-motivation
1.Unconscious incompetence	You do not know what you do not know	

Alternatively, do you remember changing cars and having to retrain yourself to switch on the lights without having to think where the switch was? Getting to do these things at the 'unconscious competence' level involves building a new neural pathway in your brain.

As you climb the learning ladder from rung 1–4 gradually becoming more capable, you may discover that in the example 'you have driven 20 miles on a motorway yet not recall the journey in detail'. Yet, you have driven the car safely and competently.

Two types of learning

If you are really in tune with your needs, you will find it easier to tackle the kind of learning involved in raising your EQ. We have suggested that there are two basic types of learning:

- **Cognitive:** Cognitive learning is about absorbing new data and gaining insights into existing frameworks of association. You also need to engage that part of the brain where your emotional signature is stored. Changing habits, such as learning to approach people positively rather than avoiding them or to give them feedback skilfully, is much more challenging than simply adding new data to old.
- **Emotional:** Emotional learning involves this and more. Emotional learning involves new ways of thinking and acting

that are more in tune with our identity – our values and beliefs and attitudes. Experiential learning is more impactful since participants connect emotionally often without even knowing or naming what they feel. However, when they engage in a meaningful experience something is more likely to shift in their amygdala. If you are told to learn a new word processing program, you will probably get on with it; however, if you are told that you need to improve control of your temper, you are likely to be upset or offended. The prospect of needing to develop greater emotional intelligence is likely to generate resistance to change. It requires changes to the connections and associations made in the brain (see the section on emotional memory in Tuesday).

We will cover learning records and more suggestions for resources on Saturday.

When you get emotionally hijacked

Consider this. You've had a long and exhausting day visiting some stunning country on holiday. You arrive back to enjoy an excellent meal, but retire early and fall into a deep sleep. Suddenly wide awake, you sit bolt upright to be confronted with a tiger so close that all you can see are its eyes. You have an immediate and very strong emotional reaction, which causes you to do one of three things (and maybe some others too!):

- you freeze
- you leap out of bed and run like mad
- you throw something at the offending animal.

You have just experienced an amygdala hijack: Flight or Fight or Freeze. Early humans relied on this reaction for their survival when confronted with danger. If Darwin is correct, we are the progeny of those ancestors who utilized the reaction successfully and survived, unlike the inflexible rest of humanity who did not adapt.

Let us look at what happened. Your reaction is an instantaneous adrenaline-based reaction and has no cognition [thinking] associated with it.

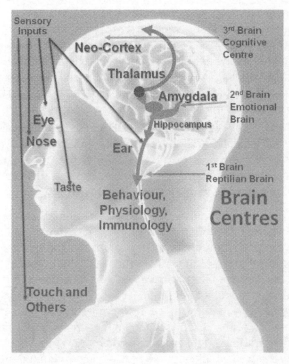

Brain centres

It is an emotional hijack because the 2nd Brain (the limbic centre) processes reactions some 80,000 times faster than the neo-cortex processes thoughts (the 3rd Brain, the cognitive centre which was the most recent to develop in mankind).

> *'In moments of emergency, our emotional centres (the limbic brain) commandeer the rest of the brain... There's good reason for this special potency of emotions. They're crucial for survival, being the brain's way of alerting us to something urgent and offering an immediate plan for action: fight, flee, freeze.'*
>
> Daniel Goleman in *Primal Leadership* (2002).

How can we take advantage of this faster processing in modern times? Ignoring gut instinct is artificial but we sometimes feel pressured to leave emotions out of decisions. Yet the greater the decisions using wide-ranging sources of data (emotional, intuitive) as well as the traditional hard (cognitive, knowledge) information, the better. It is powerful when we pick up information from all our senses and use it more perceptively to manage situations, envision the future, balance physiology, engender strong relationships and navigate social situations.

Implications in a business environment

In summary, to survive we developed a reaction that was appropriate to the situations that ancient man encountered when physically threatened. Let us consider the potential inappropriateness of this automatic response in modern business. You are likely to have had several close-call threat situations causing an adrenaline-rush. When the boss says, 'I want to see you in my office in five minutes'; do we carefully consider all of the reasons why? No, we immediately assume we are in trouble... and panic causing an emotional hijack.

Now that your thinking brain has been commandeered, your body is primed for action and is reacting with the fight reactions of anger, aggression and hostility or the flight/freeze emotions of fear, anxiety and nervousness. It is stressful not to be able to release the fight or flight energy provided, through expected physical activity. A repeated lack of release causes many illnesses with time.

Today, there are comparatively fewer real threats to our personal safety. The main threats that we perceive are of a financial, emotional, mental and social nature which can still trigger this ancient survival mechanism. These types of threats are not generally processed immediately by the brain and the effects can linger, build on each other and cause strain.

How will it change me?

Developing higher emotional intelligence implies root and branch change but you may feel better mentally and physically. However, it would also be perfectly normal to relapse back into some unhelpful behaviour – but you would have better information about the lapse and be able to prevent a recurrence. People might say that you look less stressed or that you do not overreact and you may feel more grown up and happier.

Symptoms of low EQ

We are worried, anxious and confused about priorities.

We are time-pressured, inefficient and perform poorly.

We are tired, fatigued and frustrated.

We have a poor work–life balance.

We may have elevated blood pressure.

We age more quickly.

How and why to keep a journal

Raising your EQ to reduce and eliminate unproductive behaviour is rarely completed in one giant step. With low self-awareness, development of any kind is difficult; but learning better self-awareness is something that is notoriously complex to train people into. It has to be part of a developmental process over a sensible period of time, usually following a cyclical pattern of input, reflection and discovery.

I recommend that you start a journal (on your smartphone or other readily available item); the idea is to consistently log your learning, to make this as easy as possible to store and retrieve and keep the information in one place, readily to hand. Keeping the journal will allow you to prepare for meetings – noting your feelings, thoughts or expectations of each event.

Making a record while the memory is fresh will give you the benefit of higher-quality reflection. Stick to keeping the journal; it takes three weeks to form a good habit.

If you use the following format with some academic rigour, you might be able to include the material as part of a suitable qualification (such as for management development or organizational development).

Journal format

The journal chronicles the steps on the route. General rules are to:

● Date the entry, giving qualitative details of the environment and experience.
● Give some context (why, where and with whom).
● Give anything relevant about the timing, such as an appraisal interview.
● Note anything that distracts you (you may be participating in a meeting, listening to a presentation or giving a coaching session, etc.).
● Note anything that interferes with your relationship(s) with other participants and with your role (chairperson, coach, etc.).

Each day's exercises are designed to deepen your understanding throughout and at the end of each day. You have to *feel* the difference between emotionally intelligent behaviour and undeveloped behaviour.

Most managers I have worked with say that it is only when they look back that they can distinguish their former way of being around people.

Activity: the cost of low EQ

Think for a moment of three examples where you had a strong emotional response to how you were handled, for example:

● in a face-to-face encounter as a customer with a supplier (such as with a shop assistant)
● by unsolicited email or through an unexpected telephone conversation
● contacting your service provider to access a service and getting a Customer Centre.

Write down in your journal the emotions you experienced and whether there were any flashbacks to previous experiences:

● How did you respond to or behave towards them?
● How did you feel afterwards?
● Was there any further action or reaction (e.g. a letter of praise or complaint)?

Make a journal entry with the results, which will be useful in subsequent chapters.

If your immediate response to this is that you are too busy and this request is irrelevant to your life, then I ask you to question your priorities. Leaders involved in successful change efforts have avoided the 'traps' of satisfying their own ego needs and being blind to organizational systems involved in change. Commonly, these successful individuals display a range of behaviours that demonstrate high levels of self-awareness and an ability to 'work in the here and now'. In addition, they have an ability to remain in tune with the overall purpose of the change.

Summary

This chapter has covered:

- Pessimism or optimism as components in our 'explanatory style', recognizing that we have the option to change
- A milestone history of EI-related concepts offering us the opportunity to satisfy any academic curiosity about concepts related to EI and accepted theories by following up the details
- Measurement of EQ – a list of assessments up to date at the time of writing (2011) as a choice on which to base our development of emotional intelligence, with feedback from others or a self-assessment or not
- Identifying the benefits of 'Emotional Fitness'
- That EI is learnable – understanding different learning types, stages, and how emotional learning is different
- Identifying what happens when you are emotionally hijacked – learning about a survival instinct, flight or fight
- Exploring 'how will it change me?'
- Learning how and why to keep a journal

Questions (answers at the back)

Check how much you can recall from studying this introductory chapter to the book by selecting the correct answer to the following questions.

1. **Pessimists are defined as:**
a) People who consistently see the adverse outcome of everything that other people do ☐
b) Individuals who explain to themselves in a negative fashion why they experience a particular event ☐
c) Individuals who generally blame themselves for negative events and who tend to believe that such events will continue indefinitely. They let such events affect many aspects of their lives, displaying what is called a *pessimistic explanatory style* ☐
d) People who consistently see other people and themselves in a negative light and never see any upside ☐

2. **Which choice below correctly identifies the three components of an explanatory style?**
a) Pessimist, optimist and cynic ☐
b) Personal, pervasive and permanent ☐
c) Permanent, persistent and pervasive ☐
d) Pessimistic, optimistic, distrustful ☐

3. **Who first identified the importance of emotional expression for survival and adaptation?**
a) Leuner in 1966 ☐
b) Goleman in 2002 ☐
c) Thorndike in 1920 ☐
d) Darwin in 1859 ☐

4. **Who was the first person or persons to use the phrase 'emotional intelligence'?**
a) Mayer & Salovey ☐
b) Caruso ☐
c) Leuner ☐
d) Daniel Goleman ☐

5. **Which list is the correct list of popular EI assessments?**
a) IQ, MQ, EQ, MICE, SEA, EI-Map, OVA-i, ECSI ☐
b) EIMSC, MISE, EQI, EQT, OAS, ECII ☐
c) PDP, OSI, MISE, MQ-i, SCEI ☐
d) EIQ, MSCEIT, MEIS, SEI, OVS, EQ-Map, EQ-i, EIA, ECI, ESCI ☐

6. **Which description is correct for feedback as described in the chapter from others as well as a self-score?**
a) Assessment gives individuals information about their own competence through self-scoring and discussion of it with managers, peers as well as seniors ☐
b) 360-degree instruments are reverse appraisal of managers by staff, plus feedback from peers as well as seniors ☐
c) Assessment gives individuals information about their own competence through self-scoring and discussion of it with staff they manage ☐
d) Information gained about competence by an occupational psychologist's discussions with staff ☐

MONDAY

Raising self-awareness

Becoming more self-aware is the cornerstone of developing strengths in any of the models of EI, in my view. Without the ability to look in the mirror, to see ourselves objectively and to see ourselves 'as others' perceive us, it is difficult to gain any benefits from more complex competencies in relationship management, conflict resolution and inspirational leadership.

A study by Hay Group in 2010, using the ESCI, shows that – out of 4,322 participants – those who demonstrated 'often or consistently' high emotional self-awareness, also displayed nine other ESCI competencies at strength. Conversely, those who displayed little emotional self-awareness showed less than one other competency at strength, often or consistently. This leads to an assertion that emotional self-awareness and emotional literacy are at the heart of EI.

This chapter focusses on becoming more self-aware as the foundation to developing higher emotional intelligence in a broad range of capacities:

- What is self-awareness?
- Self-awareness competencies
- You as a manager of others
- Creating the environment for others to succeed
- Journal entries

What is self-awareness?

Self-awareness means that you are aware of what you think and feel in the present. You may imagine yourself to be both strong and deeply in tune with your feelings, aware of others' emotions and adept at social intercourse to further your ambitions. Alternatively, you may feel that you are living a script written by someone else and that you are not in control of the outcomes in your daily life.

There are arguably three levels of awareness:

- **Awareness of the outside world** – what happens to us, what we see, hear, smell, taste and touch, a sense of time.
- **Awareness of the inside world** – physical sensations that happen in us, such as aching wrists, neck ache, seating pressure points, the feel of our skin in clothes, gut sensations and the emotions that surface in our stream of consciousness.
- **Awareness of fantasy activity** – imagination, recall, melancholy, simulation, all cerebral and limbic system activity beyond the present 'here and now'. Things that you feel, think and even emulate or simulate, but are not actually part of the 'here and now'.

As complex mammals, each of the three levels of awareness is useful to us, if not vital. When you become self-aware and emotionally literate, you are able to distinguish single emotions triggered unexpectedly by some event. This can help you become aware of a personal boundary (value judgements, what you can take and what you cannot endure). You then need to decide what to do with this insight to look after your unmet emotional needs.

If you have low self-awareness, the main learning outcome for you is to become more mindful. Mindfulness is one of the concepts that have been around in Eastern cultures for a long time. In the last decade, it has come into more frequent use in developing greater self-awareness and mental focus.

There are many definitions of it in academic papers and online. Here are two:

> ### Continuous, clear awareness of the present moment. Always returning, whether from an emotional outburst, an enjoyable fantasy or a melancholy remembrance; always returning to this present moment.
>
> (Sensei Kipp Ryodo Hawley, 2007, *Three Steps to Mindfulness: Bringing Zen Awareness Into Your Life*)

> ### The clear and single-minded awareness of what happens to us and in us at each successive moment of perception
>
> (Nyanaponika, 1972)

Therefore, taking this definition, examples in modern life of the opposite of being mindful and usefully self-aware are:

- Sitting at the dinner or kitchen table with the family with your smartphone next to your dinner plate. The phone constantly makes noises announcing the receipt of texts and other alerts. You do not make much conversation with the other people present. You do not listen attentively to what the others are saying. Conflict arises and you withdraw, either physically leaving the table or you start texting people or playing games.
- Driving for 20 miles along a familiar route or motorway without any conscious awareness of operating the car and completely ignoring the passenger next to you, who is trying to take some time with you to discuss issues concerning him or her.
- While in the shower, forgetting how many times you have shampooed your hair or which parts of you still need soaping.

In these examples, your focus of attention is elsewhere; you may be thinking about past, recent or future situations, conversations, observations of other people's behaviour. However, the examples are not a considerate display of empathy and respect for others – who you are believed to love, such as your husband, lover, father or sibling, and so on.

The self-aware thing to do would be to take time out in order to reflect on what is going on that leads you to behave this way. Looking at the earlier examples of the family around the table and the car journey, your relationships need to be discussed, including *your* relationship with *you*! This means developing your existing social intellect, which can be turned inwards to understand and manage yourself. After discovering what drives you in relationships, you can improve your social intelligence with others.

The latter example of forgetfulness in the shower may be indicative of how stressed you are.

● Is your response to admonish yourself?
● Does it lead to negative self-talk and put-downs?

The Wednesday chapter covers stress management and identifying sources of stress, which can include your own lack of self-regard.

Self-awareness competencies

A simple view of what it takes to be self-aware is summarized in the following.

Awareness of feelings: This is recognizing one's emotions and their effects. People with this competence:

● know which emotions they are feeling, can say why and label them
● realize the chain from emotion to action (links between their feelings and what they think, do and say)
● recognize how their feelings affect their performance, the quality of experience at work and in relationships
● have a guiding awareness of their values or goals and any gap between espoused values and actual behaviour.

Personal insight: This is knowing one's key strengths and frailties. People with this competence are:

- aware of their strengths, weaknesses and emotional boundaries in relationships
- reflective, understanding the power of learning from experience even if reflection is not their natural style
- open to candid feedback, new perspectives, continuous learning and self-development
- objective about feedback from others and able to generate positive strokes for themselves appropriately
- able to show a sense of humour and perspective about themselves.

Self-assurance: This is sureness about one's self-worth and capabilities. People with this competence:

- present themselves with self-assurance; have 'poise' with warmth
- can celebrate diversity in teams, voice views that are unpopular and go out on a limb for what is right
- are decisive, able to make sound judgements using emotional and cognitive information despite uncertainties (perceptions of risk) and pressures
- are generally recognized as self-confident.

Your learning curve from self-awareness to social adeptness may include the following:

- To be self-aware, you need to be emotionally literate. This means being able to distinguish and label accurately individual emotions (see Tuesday).
- You then learn to increase your choices of behaviour in given situations.
- Gradually, you become increasingly capable of self-control regardless of the emotions triggered by a situation.
- You can go on developmentally to use this to become more aware of others, their triggers and the emotional roots of their unhelpful behaviours.
- Finally, as you choose to develop, you become very socially adept at using your self-awareness, self-regulation and awareness of others.

You may elect to go on further, acquiring knowledge about different cultures and customs. A goal may be to manage your reaction to unexpected clashes in moral, ethical and socio-cultural standards.

Exercise – self-awareness competencies

Note the answers to the following in your journal:

- Which of the self-awareness competencies do you feel represent your strengths?
- Why?
- How do you feel about those competencies?

How would you practise and develop them:

- at home?
- in life?
- at work?

Create a list of times in terms of being self-assured when you are out of sorts and do not perform at your best. Treat this as a list of things that you choose to complete to eradicate your self-doubt. It could be that you write down items that cause you to be under-confident due to issues such as:

- relationships with crossed transactions
- misconceptions
- unchecked assumptions about people or events
- unresolved upsets.

Become aware of whether your lack of self-confidence allows you to avoid being accountable or to procrastinate. Catch yourself in the act.

If you defer decisions, make yourself think it through, write down the pros and cons.

Write down who is impacted and how they would feel.

Are you showing a lack of respect for others? Is that what you really want to happen – people to feel disrespected by you?

Realize the consequences of your lack of self-belief. This may help you to motivate yourself to eradicate negative beliefs.

Are you letting down others by doubting your self-worth and capabilities?

Are you playing the victim?

If you developed increased self-awareness, what impact and effect would it have:

SUNDAY
MONDAY
TUESDAY
WEDNESDAY
THURSDAY
FRIDAY
SATURDAY

- at work?
- at home?
- in relationships?

Think about such things as:

- being aware that you feel uncomfortable around a person, although not necessarily being able to identify why
- being aware that you are behaving badly – repeating a pattern of unhelpful behaviour
- in the car, becoming aware of your present driving style and the impact it is having on other motorists
- being aware that you are starting down a well-worn path and are unable to stop it.

Write down at least two instances of the same pattern and we will use this insight and discovery about yourself in the next chapter.

While it only takes a short time to read each chapter, you should set aside some time to run through each of the exercises. If you hesitate over this as a priority, ask someone you trust about your personal case for doing so.

You as a manager of others

Being in a state of consciousness where the mind is away from the 'here and now' is not necessarily a bad thing in the *right* context. Consider the role of imagination – the human capacity to invent entirely new worlds in one's own head. This capacity can be extremely useful in, for example:

- developing intellectual property, inventions
- problem solving and simulating solutions
- creativity in an entrepreneurial context
- originating works, fiction, films, theatre, TV series, etc.

Moreover, in the context of developing better self-awareness and other facets of emotional intelligence, imagination is extremely useful in rehearsing interactions and reactions prior to important events. However, for a manager whose role it is to get work done by others, allowing your imagination or that of a staff member to wander tends to be a distraction from performing assigned tasks. It also may be happening a lot more often than you realize and may be a sign of issues that you need to coach your staff through.

Self-assessment questions	Your answers
Do you consider yourself to be an aspiring or junior manager?	
Do you see your career progressing to leading others?	
Are you more interested in remaining solely as a technical resource without supervision responsibilities? Can you say why this is a preference?	
Have you been managed by someone with excellent people management skills? Can you describe how this felt and identify what was excellent about it?	
Which characteristics in people who influence you beneficially do you admire?	
If you have decided that you want to take a career path that will include managing other people, which qualities do you feel that you have now that are a strength, and which qualities do you feel that you may want to develop?	
What have been your most powerful learning experiences?	
How easy do you find it to stay focussed on the 'here and now' and not get distracted?	
How easy do you find it to form new habits and patterns of behaviour?	
Are you able to label emotions and chains of emotions that you experience, e.g. jealousy can be envy and anger?	
How easy do you find it to concentrate on the emotional content of conversations with others?	
If you could go back to your childhood, what messages would you pass on to benefit your younger self?	

Have a look at the table. This exercise involves answering the questions about your aspirations as a manager, the kind of role models you have encountered and your current level of self-awareness.

Journal entry: You should take time to complete a journal entry as you reflect on your answers and what insights you have gained.

Creating the environment for others to succeed

You will find that there is much debate about leadership versus management and many accepted theories about both. However, when you break it down to the fundamental benefit of hiring or promoting a person to a managerial role, it is to ensure that *other people* carry out tasks; the *right* work, being done *correctly* and *on time* for *valid* reasons including profit. The role is not to increase the status of an individual and at the same time for them to do all the work themselves.

The major finding of a report to government by David MacLeod and Nita Clarke entitled 'Engaging for Success: enhancing performance through employee engagement' was that line managers are key to employees' engagement. In 2009, an organization called 'The Engage Group' carried out research across the private and public sector to establish what approaches to employee engagement make the most impact. Employees want:

- change to be managed extremely well
- to feel more empowered
- to understand their contribution to the strategy
- to be motivated and inspired to do their best work
- to be treated fairly and to feel proud to tell others where they work.

In creating the environment for others to succeed, what does this mean for you? Who or what will you have 'to do or be' in order to achieve the right climate at work? George Litwin and Robert Stringer thought about this and published *Motivation and Organizational Climate* in 1968 and it is widely used today in managerial and organizational development work. Essentially, they measured people's collective perception of what it was like to work in an organization using measurable properties of the climate at work. They also developed models of six leadership styles that were commonly deployed in different situations to get the job done most effectively. They defined the properties of a positive organizational climate as one with the following:

- *flexibility*, where employees feel free to innovate
- where employees feel *unencumbered* by red tape
- a strong sense of *responsibility to* the organization
- clarity about the level of *standards* that people set
- confidence in the *accuracy* about performance feedback and the *aptness* of rewards
- where employees feel there is *clarity* about mission and values
- where there is a sense of the degree of *commitment to* a *common purpose*.

Taken from *Motivation and Organizational Climate*,
George Litwin and Robert Stringer

Litwin & Stringer also developed models of six leadership styles that were commonly deployed in different situations to get the job done most effectively. The assertion of a Hay McBer study run in 2010, that self-awareness is the cornerstone to having other ESCI strengths, also identifies a relationship with leadership styles. Apparently, a manager's behaviour accounts for up to 70 per cent of variability of corporate climate. Those successful managers with ten or more ESCI strengths deploy a wide range of leadership styles, which can be utilized appropriately with different demands, in a similar manner to picking a different tool for specific tasks and conditions at the time of use. This is in line with Ken Blanchard's situational leadership model and he advises managers to:

- open up communication – increase the frequency and quality of conversations about performance and development
- coach others to develop both competence and commitment
- teach others self-directed learning skills, how to provide their own direction and support
- value and honour differences.

In sharp contrast, those with low self-awareness showed a consistent use of the coercive leadership style, which creates a negative organizational climate. Managers using this style alone fail to get highly engaged employees. Highly engaged employees create the greatest value for companies: very satisfied clients, many referrals and good word-of-mouth, good revenues, goodwill and so on. Therefore, if you are on the first rung of the management ladder, becoming more self-aware will be an invaluable asset to your ability to inspire others to perform well.

You need to see yourself as others see you and this process involves organising a process of getting objective feedback; the absence of which can lead to blind spots in your leadership effectiveness.

Blind spots may lead to frustration for you and your team and impact on the organization adversely.

Conversely, receiving 360-degree (all round) feedback from employees, peers, clients, suppliers and other significant relationships for your role, you will have a rich source of developmental advice based on evidence (often processed objectively by an external coach or occupational psychologist).

Initially, it may be uncomfortable or hard to accept this type of 'reports from others' about your behaviour and apparent attitudes at work. It can feel like a real threat in your work environment. However, with practice and encouragement, you will survive the process and adapt your ability to learn from feedback. I have experienced all of these uncomfortable feelings – even though I was the one who initiated a 360-degree leadership report after leading a large team of 40 people on a high-pressure project. However, I knew it would be the best opportunity ever to learn about myself and my impact on others. So essentially, I wanted to be authentic as a person brought in to manage others in a pressurised programme launching a new organisation into the commercial world.

Authentic leadership was first written about in *Why should anyone be led by you?* by Rob Goffee and Gareth Jones following their research at the London Business School. They wrote about what it takes to be an authentic leader. The messages are all about emotional intelligence; you need to know yourself and to be yourself, with the EI skill to understand that what works for one person will not necessarily work for another person. Goffee and Jones also talk about leadership being non-hierarchical and contextual.

Emotional learning using feedback mechanisms and monitoring behavioural change supplements what you can acquire from all other means and media: books, ebooks, traditional training, action learning, audio and other media, coaching and mentoring and so on.

Journal entries

Reflect on the following examples: Create a log in your journal.

Consider a life of being present in the 'here and now', experiencing distinct emotions, being able to label each one and to track where they came from in the past.

- Does considering this possibility make you nervous?
- Does it tempt you to make some snide remark, calling on cynicism for protection?

Consider that the most outstanding things are achieved by taking risks; in the case of emotional intelligence, by *being* differently – much more so than by *doing* anything differently.

Become aware before, during and after key events in all three aspects of consciousness.

Consider the third level of awareness, the fantasy element, to:

- prepare for any meetings or interviews
- visualize or simulate how the others present may be projecting my performance at the time, based on my answers to questions
- predict how the first days of a job work out.

The start of self-awareness is to test your readiness to change. Have you any motivation to change? What relevance does EI have to you? Make a note of, or tick, all the following points that apply. Developing your EQ will help you if you are concerned with:

- ❏ your influencing skills; wanting to understand others more in terms of what persuades them, what they can actively listen to and really hear
- ❏ stressful situations that get on top of you and that cause you to be anxious about them hours after they have occurred or that wake you up in the middle of the night
- ❏ getting the message across to people unambiguously and being able to listen without inner dialogue disrupting concentration
- ❏ your life–work balance because it must become more equitable and you need to renegotiate how your time is spent
- ❏ relationships that are stressful or even mystifying in terms of your behaviour or the reactions of others
- ❏ your general health being below what is accepted as a healthy norm and suspecting that it is self-inflicted injury in the form of bad habits, self-deprecation and lack of commitment.

Log in your journal any conclusions that you reach as to why EI is of particular interest and value to you from the above list and your own ideas. Leave space to log more conclusions as they occur to you throughout the week. Plan your next step for raising your EI competencies using this feedback.

When I have put myself under extreme pressure, say, changing from a perfectly successful career in the Royal Navy to a life of self-employed peaks and troughs and three recessions, the things that have got me through are my degree of self-awareness in any one situation and the strong relationships I have built with family, friends and other self-employed colleagues.

Tomorrow, we will look at increasing our self-control, building on self-awareness through the use of our inner voice.

Summary

This chapter has focussed on understanding self-awareness as the foundation to developing higher emotional intelligence in a broad range of capacities:

- Learning about definitions of self-awareness and related concepts, exploring self-awareness and mindfulness plus modern life examples of a lack of awareness
- Identifying the importance of emotions and the application of the human capacity to manage emotions to your present-day life
- Identifying your learning curve and thinking about the path you want to take and why
- Raising your self-awareness through being guided in your thinking about situations
- Testing your own readiness or willingness to change
- Learning about self-awareness capability as a manager and which traits you consider to be strengths and which may require development
- Looking at creating the environment for others to succeed (what does this mean you will have to do or be to achieve the right climate at work?)
- Developing a learning journal to help your development of heightened self-awareness

Questions (answers at the back)

SUNDAY
MONDAY
TUESDAY
WEDNESDAY
THURSDAY
FRIDAY
SATURDAY

1. **Those with high emotional self-awareness:**

a) Have high degrees of self-motivation ☐

b) Are individuals with attributes that consistently or often experience events in a positive fashion ☐

c) Demonstrate 'often or consistently' nine other ESCI competencies at strength ☐

d) Consistently see other people and themselves in a positive light and never see any downside ☐

2. **Successful managers with ten or more ESCI strengths:**

a) Deploy their preferred leadership styles consistent with their personality ☐

b) Deploy a wide range of leadership styles, which can be utilized appropriately with different demands ☐

c) Deploy consistently or often the coercive style of leadership to meet deadlines at work ☐

d) Develop a leadership style specifically matched to the organizational climate ☐

3. **Managers with low self-awareness:**

a) Can demonstrate flexibility in how they handle staff ☐

b) Deploy their preferred leadership styles consistent with their personality ☐

c) Utilize their experience in how they were brought up to deal with their staff ☐

d) Show a consistent use of the coercive leadership style, which creates a negative organizational climate ☐

4. **The components of a positive climate at work were developed by:**

a) Mayer, Salovey & Caruso ☐

b) Daniel Goleman ☐

c) Litwin & Stringer ☐

d) Professor David McClelland ☐

5. **Which list is the correct précis of the components of a positive climate at work?**

a) Flexibility, adaptability, sense of authority, clarity about quality, accuracy in performance feedback, and the aptness of rewards ☐

b) Flexibility, unencumbered by red tape, sense of responsibility, clarity about standards, accuracy in performance feedback, and the aptness of rewards ☐

c) Freedom of expression, unencumbered by red tape, reliability, clarity about performance, accuracy in pay and remuneration, and the aptness of the mission ☐

d) Flexibility, adaptability and readiness for change, sense of respect for others, clarity about supervision, accuracy in performance feedback, and the aptness of rewards ☐

Raising
self-control

What you will learn in this chapter is how to focus on the use of raised self-awareness (covered on Monday) in order to break unhelpful habits, form new ones and have enhanced self-regulation. This is important to aspiring or junior managers as supervision of others requires an individual to be self-aware, in control of his or her reactions and able to get inside the shoes of staff under his or her leadership. Overall, the content of this chapter is to learn about the mechanisms of self-control and consciousness to take control of behavioural patterns.

This involves laying the groundwork in understanding some concepts:

The mechanisms of self-control and consciousness

Taking control of your behavioural patterns

Our memory

Pattern matching and the APET model

Competencies for self-control

Becoming emotionally literate

Journal entries and activities

The mechanisms of self-control and consciousness

It is useful as an aspiring or junior manager to have more insight into the workings of your own brain as well as having a greater understanding of others. Understanding the physiology of the brain and the mind/body link helps us understand the emotional roots to behaviour and the impact of the subconscious mind.

If you have ever experienced extreme situations, you may have been surprised that your body carried out some actions without much conscious intervention at the time. Some of the mystifying things that we do in crises may have been stored and remembered without conscious thought; hence, we reflect in hindsight on what happened as opposed to being able to change our actions in the 'here and now'.

It is vital to understand the emotional roots to our behaviour if self-directed change is to be successful and for us to become skilled at self-control. It is also important to have knowledge of recent neuroscience, which has identified that emotional memories and memories about emotions are processed differently by the brain. The mechanisms of self-control and consciousness relating to emotional memory are explained further in the following paragraphs and diagrams.

Brain centres

The limbic system (2nd brain, emotional brain – see diagram in Sunday) developed in our distant mammalian ancestors to deal with instinctive behaviours, such as eating, drinking, mating, defending ourselves and surviving. The amygdala consists of two almond-shaped structures in the limbic region (it is so-named because amygdala is the Greek word for almond). In essence, the amygdala promotes survival; it is continually scanning the environment and interpreting each new stimulus in terms of whether it is safe or suspect. Consequently, many of our body's alarm circuits are grouped together in the amygdala because of evolution; many sensory inputs converge in the amygdala, using multiple sensory inputs to inform it of potential dangers in its environment. This sensory information comes to the amygdala either directly from the sensory thalamus or from the various sensory cortices.

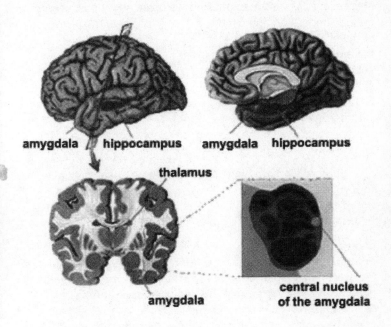

The amygdala

The amygdala appears to involve identifying stimuli that are potentially threatening the organism using intense personal recollection of emotional memories and it is essential in decoding emotions. As author and psychologist Daniel Goleman describes it, the emotional brain commandeers the neo-cortex and very quickly begins to blank out the more subtle distinctions between stimuli. When making a life-saving decision, our capacity to discern finer detail is unavailable. In fact, all thoughts and perceptions are preceded by emotions; this often subtle process is out of conscious awareness. However, the fact remains that thoughts are carried aloft on emotion.

The amygdala triggers the physiological 'fight or flight' response, thinking only in stark survival-type choices:

● Fight (will I win against this specific threat?) Or
● Flight (am I faster than it?) Or
● Freeze (if I do not respond, will it stop seeing me as prey?).

In colloquial terms, the amygdala asks:

● Can I approach this or not?
● Can I eat this or will it eat me?
● Will I fight and win, or should I flee?
● If I freeze, will it leave me alone or not see me in the undergrowth?

You may not have been confronted by a tiger (predator) at close quarters before, but you will have had several close-call situations which have caused an adrenaline-rush. You know the feeling: thumping heart, eyes wide open (to take in as much information as possible), churning stomach, your whole body focussed on one thing, and a knee-jerk reaction, possibly in this case – flight.

● At the moment of seeing the tiger, you moved from a state of low arousal to one of very high arousal caused by the flood of adrenaline (or noradrenaline) released into your system.
● Your reaction is based on experience of the same or similar situations. It is instantaneous and has no cognitive thought associated with it. It is a hijack because the amygdala is reacting at 80,000 times faster than the cognitive part of the brain, so it is difficult to overcome the rapid adrenaline-based reaction.

Are you reacting to someone at work in this way? The amygdala hijack is not saving your life in this case. Yet, are we creating an 'office tiger'? The degree to which the fight or flight reflex is activated is the degree to which our thinking becomes polarized – more black or more white. The job of the conscious mind (3rd brain, neo-cortex) is to discriminate, to fill in details and to offer a more subtle intelligent analysis of the patterns offered up by the emotional brain; in other words, shades of grey and not just black or white. However, the logic of the emotional brain has a more basic pattern going back to our distant ancestors' earliest life forms. This basic pattern still forms the foundation on which much of our thinking and behaviour rests today.

Much of this knowledge about brain function has come from the scientific study and research using individuals with known brain function damage, injury or disease:

● If the pattern-matching process is disrupted because of minor brain damage, this means that the neo-cortex can no longer draw on emotional memories from the limbic system. Therefore, sufferers believe that family and close friends are impostors, because they experience no feelings for them.
● Some recent studies have shown that amygdala damage results in problems in recognizing facial expressions of fear, anger and disgust and interferes with social and emotional judgement. In one study designed to test individuals' ability to make judgements about the approachability of people they were shown in photographs, researchers found that those with damage to the amygdala were much more likely to rate people as approachable, regardless of fearsome looks, which in healthier individuals would generate a threat response.

Taking control of your behavioural patterns

It is the *inappropriate* triggering of this system for survival, which needs to be the focus of our development of self-control and, in the next chapter, our development of stress management strategies. The different stages of self-control development involve moving from hindsight, through mid-sight to foresight such that the emotional roots to behaviour can be predicted.

Instinctive reaction comes from the 3rd brain (the reptilian brain) and involves no thinking (cognition) at all. When the hairs on the back of your neck stand up, this is the reptilian brain in action.

Hindsight comes from the 2nd brain (affect) because your thalamus and amygdala hijacked the stimuli before the neo-cortex had a chance to form thoughts.

Mid-sight also occurs when your development is progressing towards foresight and it involves being able to avoid an amygdala hijack or to quickly recover from one to bring yourself back into coherence.

Foresight comes from the 3rd brain or neo-cortex (cognition) working with the limbic system coherently. Your brain and physiology have to be coherent with each other to be able to predict reactions and choose alternative behaviour.

Thus, emotion appears to be a precondition for thought and perception even in cases when we perceive that no emotion is involved at all.

We can train ourselves to react differently, to react positively, and to use foresight rather than hindsight to manage our emotions. To be successful in this, we need to rehearse acquiring foresight frequently so that we become unconsciously competent in it. At this point, we react in a different manner without really thinking about it. Just like switching on the lights of our new car without fumbling.

Therefore, to manage our emotions we need to take control of our behaviours. To do that we must first recognize the emotional roots: certain behaviours are generally associated with specific emotions. For example, we approach people when we are enthusiastic, we sit around and do nothing when we are depressed and we fidget when anxious.

These are of course generalizations. If the behaviours go unchecked, they perpetuate negative emotions. Often we do not notice our own behaviour. A raised voice in response to anger or excitement means that we may not even be aware that we are doing it. If you want to change a situation of never or rarely being able to manage unhelpful responses, emotions or impulses, you are going to have to:

- understand the cost to you of the related anxiety and stress and decide that you do not want to pay this price any longer
- understand the triggers that are unique to you as an individual
- commit to more reflection on your behaviour.

Initially, this will be with more hindsight but with practice, you will catch yourself in the middle. Eventually, you will achieve foresight about unhelpful impulses and bad habits before you act on them.

Our memory

In order for us to gain this understanding and to improve our self-directed development, we need to utilize our human capacity for managing emotions. This in turn requires us to have knowledge of the different mechanisms for storing and recalling memories and to understand the different ways in which emotional memories are formed and stored.

Most people are aware that they have a short-term memory system and a long-term memory system. The human brain has a number of centres involved in what we commonly call our memory.

- **Episodic memory** is the memory of events, times, places, associated emotions and other contextual knowledge that can be explicitly stated, known as autobiographical events.
- **Semantic memory** refers to the memory of meanings, understandings and other concept-based knowledge unrelated to specific experiences. Semantic memory includes generalized knowledge that does not involve memory of a specific event. The conscious recollection of facts and information or general knowledge about the world is generally thought to be independent of context and personal relevance. For instance, you can answer a question like 'Are wrenches pets or tools?' without remembering any specific event in which you learned that wrenches are tools.
- **Declarative memory or explicit memory:** together, semantic and episodic memory make up one of the two major divisions in memory, the category called 'declarative memory'.
- **Procedural memory or implicit memory** is the counterpart to declarative memory, such things as playing the piano, knowing how to ride a bike or the process of using a tool. Procedural memory does not appear to involve the hippocampus; instead, it appears to be associated with modifications in the cerebellum, the basal ganglia and the motor cortex, all of which are involved in motor control. As evidence to this effect, procedural memory is not affected by amnesia caused by lesions to the hippocampus, but it is affected by damage to the cerebellum and by neurodegenerative diseases.

The formation of new episodic memories requires the medial temporal lobe, a structure that includes the hippocampus. Without the medial temporal lobe, one is still able to form new procedural memories but cannot remember the events during which they happened.

From three months after conception until five-years-old, all of a human's physical body states are stored in the amygdala together with the perceptual contexts, which accompanied the states. The reasons why we do not remember traumas experienced very early in our lives is explained by the parallel operation of our **explicit** (hippocampal) and **implicit** (amygdalic) memory systems. In infancy, while the amygdala is already able to record unconscious memories at that age, the hippocampus is still immature.

The amygdala performs two processes:

- to store any novel physical body state with its associated perceptual context
- to re-trigger the associated physical body state when presented with a familiar perceptual context during a later episode.

Approximately at the age of five, the amygdala stops the first process and continues the second retriggering process for the remainder of that person's life.

For example, if a pregnant mother slipped and became frightened, the physiological state of the mother (such well-known defence reactions as a pounding heart, muscle tension, bodily changes, inhibition, flight, preparation for defensive attack) is experienced in the womb by the baby. The physical body states associated with fright are then stored in the baby's amygdala along with the perceptual context of the falling motion when its mother slipped. During a subsequent slip, through its associative learning of a conditioned fear, the baby may experience the same body state (pounding heart, etc.) regardless of whether the mother does or not. The fright response is triggered automatically by the baby's amygdala.

Thus, early childhood traumas can disturb the mental, physiological and behavioural functions of adults by mechanisms that they cannot access consciously. This same pounding heart may be experienced 30 or 40 years later when as an airline passenger you experience momentary flight turbulence, mimicking the original prenatal slip. However, this similar perceptual context and the accompanying physical body state are experienced and associated now as a 'fear of flying'.

The hippocampus is also especially sensitive to the encoding of the context associated with an adverse experience. It is because of the hippocampus that not only can a stimulus become a source of conditioned fear, but also all the objects surrounding it will become associated plus the situation or location in which it occurs.

Because the neo-cortex evolved out of the emotional brain, there are innumerable connections between the two; more extending upwards than extending downwards. Thus, this gives the emotional brain enormous influence over mood, how we think as well as feel.

However, the limbic system developed a rudimentary ability for memory and learning to avoid going on full alert each time the senses detected a source of danger. It needed to be able to recognize which stimuli are threats and which are not; a process that we term pattern matching, which still underlies our mental functioning today.

Many other structures in the limbic system also help to encode our long-term memories. Housed in the limbic system, the emotional centre of the brain developed some millions of years before the neo-cortex; the latter being the highest part of our brains which is concerned with thinking, planning, memory, and other functions. The limbic system is concerned with raw emotion; it is the higher centres that put a more delicate spin on things, enlarging pleasure and desire into a capacity to bond with and care for other human beings, for instance.

Pattern matching and the APET model

The more complex the life form, the more rich and varied are the instinctive templates laid down and the more flexibility available to it to complete the template pattern in the live environment. All mammals are programmed with species-appropriate instinctive behaviours during REM sleep while still foetuses in the womb. REM sleep accounts for a high proportion of sleep in foetuses and newborns and drops off markedly as an organism starts to mature.

The laying down of instinctive templates at these times explains all our species-specific behaviours, such as birds' ability to know what materials to use to build nests, wild animals' ability to recognize a predator, and babies' knowledge of the need to locate the nipple and to search out human faces to establish bonding. However, these instinctive patterns cannot be too specific. They need to be flexible enough to enable them to be completed in different ways in different environments.

Therefore, a baby fawn (deer) will recognize a range of the kinds of sounds that its mother may make. A human baby will accept the teat of a bottle from which to take milk.

Infants will be able to speak the language that they hear around them, whatever it is, and their soft palate will adapt to the range of sounds expected of them (which can be heard when individuals speak with a foreign accent in your native language).

The pattern-matching process is, then, an instinctive part of human brain functioning where we map new frameworks into old. The pattern-matching process is behind our natural inclination to describe one thing in terms of another ('Such and such is like ...') and express ourselves in metaphor.

Dreams have been shown to be exact pattern matches or metaphors for emotionally arousing concerns from the day that have not been expressed before bedtime. The often-strange scenarios we dream during REM sleep at night are metaphorical renderings of those concerns which serve to deactivate them (this is not the same as resolving them).

Thus, emotional arousal in the brain is reduced and we are freed to deal with whatever demands the next day brings. So the same process, REM sleep, that first programmes instinctive behaviour in the form of genetically anticipated patterns, is also the means by which 'left-over' patterns of stimulation from waking are deactivated each night.

Pattern matching is what an animal's emotional brain uses when a tree looms into view and is recognized not to be a threat or when a certain other animal appears and is instantly deemed to be one, that is, a predator. As we have said, this 'threat/no threat' response is resolved within the first few milliseconds of the stimulus having been perceived. With the development of the neo-cortex and reason (the 3rd brain), we humans now have a much *greater range* of responses available to us when presented with stimuli in the environment.

The thinking was that the neo-cortex moderated emotional responses, bringing more diversity of reasoning to a strange situation – the knowledge, for instance, that the man seemingly blatantly blocking the path of our car is not an aggressor but is a traffic policeman doing his job. However, when the stimulus is one that causes *significant* emotional arousal (something crashes to the ground and we jump aside), the thinking brain has no role at all in the instantaneous reaction. It is the amygdala in the 2nd brain that pattern-matches and reacts *before* the neo-cortex in the 3rd brain 'even gets a look in'.

This is a relatively recent finding; the emotional brain's ability to be one jump ahead of the neo-cortex was the discovery of researcher Joseph LeDoux. It has a great bearing on the evolution of practice using the APET model by Joe Griffin and Ivan Tyrell of the European Therapy Studies Institute which replaced the ABC Model of cognitive behavioural therapy. LeDoux found that certain fear signals from the senses, once relayed to the thalamus, are immediately sent along a neuronal 'fast track' to the amygdala, arriving half a second before signals relayed by the usual route reach the neo-cortex. That half a second is a long time in brain response terms and in terms of surviving or not.

The APET model acknowledges the order in which we now know the different stages of perception and evaluation actually happen. Black and white thinking, which underlies all the categories identified by cognitive therapists, is the thinking style of the emotional brain. It is the result of arousal, and the accompanying hijacking of the neo-cortex, not the cause of the arousal.

The APET model takes into account the latest neuroscience knowledge about how the human brain works and uses it for more effective development.

The **A** in APET stands for activating agent: any event or stimulus in the environment, just as in the cognitive model. Information about that stimulus, taken in through the senses, is processed through the pattern-matching part of the mind (**P**), which gives rise to an emotion (**E**) which *may* inspire certain thoughts (**T**).

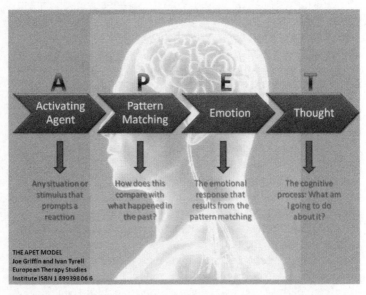

The APET model (J. Griffin and I. Tyrell, European Therapy Studies Institute)

Some implications are:

- Communication with someone in a state of high emotional arousal is impaired. Only when a person is calm can their neo-cortex employ the subtle 'shades of grey' thinking and reframing abilities that allow adaptation of patterns and the solving of problems. Therefore, ensuring that the person is calm is an essential precondition for effective communication to work.

- Some traumatic events are never processed in the neo-cortex to be verbalized and rationalized. Any recall of the traumatic event simply triggers the emotional and physiological responses again. Thus, processes that encourage the person to relive or 'talk through' the incident may well make the repeated experience more intense.
- Each letter of the 'A.P.E.T. model' potentially represents a point of possible change. In some instances, it may be most effective to change the activating agent, that is, to encourage or to suggest strategies for changing an unsatisfying career or in reducing a fear of authority figures.

Emotion (the E of the model) always needs to be calmed down before anyone can learn to think in a less black and white fashion. It is impossible to communicate fully with anyone who is overly emotionally aroused, as very many of us will know from experience of arguments. Even if it is not so apparent to the onlooker, depression is equally as aroused an emotional state as anger.

Emotional arousal, with its black and white logic, is blocking access to the more subtle reasoning of people's higher brains. Thus, the depressed person thinks everything *always* goes wrong and that no relationship will *ever* work, because there are no greys in black and white thinking.

High emotional arousal locks people's focus of attention into a negative trance state where they are confined to viewing the world and their own circumstances from a limiting viewpoint. Teaching relaxation techniques and working with individuals who are in a state of deep relaxation reduces the emotional brain's paralysing hold over the neo-cortex.

Finally, it is highly valuable to work with any unhelpful thoughts or belief patterns (T) that may be holding clients back, diminishing their confidence, arousing distress or placing too great demands on them. When people are relaxed and their focus of attention is taken off their emotions, the neo-cortex can feed a new pattern back down to the emotional brain.

Consciously or out of our awareness, a thought is underpinned by an emotion or chain of emotions. Therefore, our thinking serves an emotional agenda. Thought is an evolutionary adaptation that ultimately serves to help us get our needs fulfilled – for fame and fortune, for the satisfaction of solving a mystery, for the joy of originating a new work or invention and so on.

A thought, therefore, is always the end, not the starting, point of the APET process.

Dreaming is a clear example of how the brain is always serving an emotionally driven agenda. Humans experience about five periods of REM sleep a night, during which we dream. Dreams are exact pattern matches to emotionally driven agendas that have not been completed during the day. By providing the pattern match to the emotional arousal the dream deactivates it, freeing up our thought processes to deal with whatever the new activation agents of the next day will bring.

Incorrect or inappropriate pattern matching is at the centre of most psychological disorders. The most effective treatments involve detaching old unhelpful patterns and cementing in new empowering ones.

Competencies for self-control

Over the last two decades, the role of emotion in behaviour has been and still is examined with academic rigour. Earlier in the chapter, we looked at the brain centres involved and how memory and emotion have several mechanisms in play in mammals depending on perceptions of threat. Therefore, for the purposes of self-directed learning the following competencies reflect my personal view of the next step from self-awareness to self-control. Full assessments were listed in a table in Sunday if you have decided that you wish to progress more formally using an assessment and some support.

Self-regulation: Managing emotions and holding back unhelpful impulses

To have this competency you would:

❑ Stop acting on impulse when it is an unproductive behaviour.
❑ Remain collected, positive and unflustered even at testing times.
❑ Manage distressing emotions and reduce anxiety associated with experiencing them.
❑ Think lucidly, remaining focussed under pressure.

Authenticity: Being true to yourself and others

To have this competency you would:

- ❏ Build trust through your reliability and congruent behaviour (words and actions are aligned).
- ❏ Act ethically, being above reproach and questioning of your own motives.
- ❏ Admit flaws and confront unethical actions in others (zero tolerance).
- ❏ Stand up for your values even when in the minority.
- ❏ Expect yourself to slip back occasionally and have a sense of humour and compassion about it.

Accountability: Taking responsibility, owning your performance

To have this competency you would:

- ❏ Take responsibility for your actions and inaction where appropriate.
- ❏ Clear up miscommunication and keep promises.
- ❏ Hold yourself accountable to objectives.
- ❏ Prioritize what is important and urgent every day at work.

Flexibility: Embracing and adapting to change

To have this competency you would:

- ❏ Take account of potential change in your planning.
- ❏ Be able to let go, accept shifting priorities and a challenging pace of change.
- ❏ Be adaptable in how you perceive events or different people.
- ❏ Be open to confronting change issues and exploring the personal implications.
- ❏ Be innovative to account for change, generating and sharing ideas.

Self-motivation: Positively managing your outlook

To have this competency you would:

- ❏ Be driven to improve or meet high standards.
- ❏ Demonstrate commitment in all your relationships.
- ❏ Look for the opportunity first, not the problem.
- ❏ Show persistence in pursuing goals and intentionality in overcoming barriers or setbacks.

If you tick everything in this competence, you have great emotional maturity. Developing a high EQ demands accurate self-assessment and consistent behaviour in all circumstances.

Becoming emotionally literate

Emotional literacy is the capacity to identify and label positive and negative emotions including any blanket emotions such as fear or anger, and this is a skill which can be acquired to aid the pattern-matching 'rewiring' process in development.

Becoming able to label distinct emotions accurately allows us to examine the first time we experienced those emotions. Frequently, unhelpful behaviours in adults can be linked to interpretation during some past event. We experience a chain of emotions during an incident and we make it mean something about ourselves, about our standards or place in the world.

We use the fantasy level of self-awareness (third level, see Monday) to reinterpret the facts of the incident. We then bring the story into focus and the actual facts of what occurred fade into memory.

This false interpretation is remembered and carried through inappropriately into later life. This can be recycled many times and the story grows more distant from fact.

Exercising a new muscle

To develop your self-awareness and self-control, you are going to develop a different part of your brain. It is like exercising a new muscle and it requires focus and concentration. Therefore, to help you here are a few very simple rules that you can apply quickly and easily.

- To express your thoughts, start with the words, 'I think ...'
- To express feelings, start with the words, 'I feel ...', and then add a feeling word. If you say, 'I feel *that* ...' then you are actually expressing what you *think*.
- Use the following table of emotions to expand your vocabulary of emotion-related adjectives.

Essentially, we have just four *primary* feelings: mad, sad, glad and scared. However, we use many different words to describe them at different levels of intensity.

Recognizing blanket emotions

Feelings can also be complex, known as blanket emotions, indicated by an asterisk (*) in the table. Underneath a blanket emotion are the emotional memories that give you much better insight into what is driving you. In other words, you may be behaving aggressively with someone that you love, but underneath you are afraid that they do not love you, are going to abandon you, might be in love with someone else, may humiliate you in front of friends and family, and so on. Some emotions are composites of two or more primary feelings; for example, jealousy can comprise envy, anger, fear, sadness, a sense of loss and so on. If you are to sustain beneficial changes, it is very important that you learn to distinguish the separate emotions involved in complex emotions. You must explore what might have originally triggered each one because frustration, anger and confusion do not enlighten the cause.

Mad	Sad	Glad	Scared
angry*	blue	amused	afraid
annoyed*	depressed*	comfortable	agitated
ashamed	despondent	content	alone
belittled*	discouraged	ecstatic	awkward
guilty	distressed	effervescent	concerned
irritated	down	elated	confused
jealous*	down and out	excited	distressed
disappointed	grief	fascinated	nervous
discouraged	hurt	fulfilled	forgetful
frustrated*	lonely	giddy	ignored*
furious*	left out	glorious	Inhibited

We can use our increased personal insight and ability to assess our feelings to revisit the first time these emotions were experienced, which may be before the age of five or even pre-natal as discussed earlier in the chapter.

Emotional Literacy Exercise

Make a list of all the emotions that you are likely to experience in your workplace: say, job satisfaction, anger, joy, companionship, anxiety, contentment, enthusiasm, fear, sadness and frustration.

● List which behavioural patterns accompany the emotions that you are most likely to encounter at work.
● For all of the emotions on the list, what are your corresponding actions?
● Explore any unhelpful behavioural patterns. For example, you avoid running into your boss because you are afraid you might be moved from your job.
● Look at your behavioural actions in response to other situations in your workplace. Visualizing yourself in the situation, you can re-evaluate any negative self-beliefs that were formed or beliefs about others. As the skill builds, you can then choose a new response to the chain of emotions triggered by the situation, should you encounter them again.

Journal entries and activities

You should ask a friend who knows you well to review your strengths in the self-control competencies earlier in the chapter as a way to improve areas in which you are less capable. Remember that a generic goal of exercises is to learn the process of making small changes within your own limits. The purpose is not to be perfect. Be gentle with yourself, if you are less than satisfied with the results or the speed of progression.

Exercises to generate an internal observer

You need to practise deconstructing the emotional roots of your behaviour in routine work situations. The effectiveness of meetings and their impact on stress levels is mainly due to human relationships. Prepare by reflection on past meetings, using the competencies described yesterday and today. Look at the agenda as early as possible. Routine meetings have packed agendas; however, you can still raise your self-awareness and self-control by using them as vehicles. Find out how other attendees regard agenda items in advance.

You can explain that you are doing self-development to make meetings more valuable. Log insights from reflection in your journal:

- what happened and how you felt about it.
- what went well
- what you would do differently.

Signs of low EQ to look for:

- **Diversion** – you are telling someone some details but become aware that some aspect of the communication triggers emotions, interfering with the message. For example, you become aware that your driver for this emotion is that you see this person achieving an unfulfilled ambition of yours and you feel thwarted in your own ambitions.
- **Distraction** – the body language of one or more attendees shows impatience and this non-verbal communication is transmitted and replicated by you.
- **Internal dialogue** – you drift off listening to your inner voice because some aspect of the here and now is of insufficient interest.
- **Misinterpretation** – you make things said or done in meetings mean something adverse about you whereas, in reality there is no personal inference at all.
- **Withdrawal** – Holding back or not contributing at all, these are indirect or passive aggressive behaviours.
- **Emotional outbursts** – outrageous attention-seeking behaviour! Can include the 'and another thing' monologue where strings of unmet emotional needs, often unexpressed previously, bubble to the surface and come out all at once.
- **Using humour** –to avoid debating or acknowledging some underlying issue and blanketing it from being aired.
- **Losing focus** – what obsesses or hooks you and where do you go mentally? Perhaps you have been confronted by something being acted out or said by participants. Do you retreat into self-denial, self-justification, avoidance or something else?

Tomorrow, we look at how significant a contributor developing your EI can be to your personal stress management strategies and practices.

Summary

This chapter has covered the mechanisms of self-control, consciousness and emotional memory needed to take control of behavioural patterns.

We looked at:

● Acquiring more self-control using the human capacity for associative learning and the ability to master conditioned responses

● Memory mechanisms for recording and recalling memories

● Pattern matching and a model describing human responses – the APET model gives insight to why we react as we do in adverse conditions and what we can do about it

● Competencies for self-control – the human capacity to manage emotions and any reaction to patterns of emotions

● Developing improved emotional intelligence using self-reflection (in hindsight) as part of the learning curve to moderating your own behaviour to help predict adverse reactions and prevent bad habits re-emerging

● Expressing examples of emotional awareness at different stages of development and demonstrating how to deconstruct the emotional roots of your behaviour

● Identifying which self-control competencies are strengths and which require development

● Becoming emotionally literate in order to identify blanket emotions which hinder discoveries useful to progression and how to correctly label emotions both positive and negative and in terms of their intensity

● Using journal entries for self-observation to deconstruct your own behaviour and its emotional roots

● Examples of low EQ

Questions (answers at the back)

1. **Humans have several different types of memory. Which one of the following is incorrect?**
a) Long-term memory and short-term memory ❏
b) Explicit memory and implicit memory ❏
c) Procedural memory and declarative memory ❏
d) Inner memory and outer memory ❏

2. **The emotional brain contains several elements. Which one is correct?**
a) The limbic system contains the amygdala, the thalamus and the hippocampus ❏
b) The reptilian brain, the limbic system and the cognitive centre ❏
c) The neo-cortex, primary sensory cortex and the thalamo-amygdala pathway ❏
d) The 1st, 2nd and 3rd cognitive brain centres ❏

3. **The primitive brain assesses stimuli for potential threats. The response triggered is known as the:**
a) Fright, famine or feast response ❏
b) Fight, flight or freeze response ❏
c) Fright, fight or freeze response ❏
d) Flight, fright or fight response ❏

4. **Which of the following describes the APET model?**
a) The APET model acknowledges the order of perception and evaluation ❏
b) The APET model describes the flow from the reptilian to the limbic and cognitive brain centres ❏
c) The APET model describes the flows to the neo-cortex through the thalamo-amygdala pathway ❏
d) The APET model describes the flows from the 1st brain centre, towards the 2nd and 3rd brain centres ❏

5. **The APET model moves through four steps. Select the correct description.**
a) The APET model acknowledges the order of perception and evaluation: A is the activating agent, P is the pattern-matching process, E is the emotional response and T is the thought process ❏
b) The APET model acknowledges the order of perceiving and acting: A is the affective agent, P is the perception process, E is the effective response and T is the thinking process ❏
c) The APET model describes the steps from the primary sensory cortices through the thalamo-amygdala pathway to the neo-cortex ❏
d) The APET model describes the flows from the first reptilian brain, through the second immotile brain towards the third cognitive brain centre ❏

WEDNESDAY

Stress management

The previous chapters have prepared the ground to become more self-aware and see ourselves more objectively. We have also covered some of the new knowledge that has emerged in the last two decades regarding brain function and our ability to manage emotions and use emotional memory.

Few readers are likely to dispute the assertion that the last decade has been challenging for many people in different nations across the planet. Therefore, the ability to cope in a sustainable way with externally induced stress is useful. Our ability to identify and eliminate internally focussed stress from inappropriate responses to perceived threats is vital to long-term health, physiologically and mentally.

Today, we are going to gain an understanding of the following topics:

What is stress?
The stress cycle
Stress-related illnesses
Work-life balance
Stress management strategies using EI
An EI approach to reducing stress
Journal entries

What is stress?

The word stress is derived from the Latin word *stringere*, which means to draw tight. According to Hinkle (1973), 'in the seventeenth century the word was used to describe "hardship or afflictions"'.

As we discovered on Tuesday, when threatened by a tiger (real or the office tiger) your body pumps in noradrenaline to prepare for fight or flight. Sugars, cholesterol and fatty acids are released into the bloodstream and the blood pressure and heartbeat increases.

There is an immediate and powerful mood change; you do not start smiling or laughing in these circumstances. Primed for action, the noradrenaline surge is an 'upper' to optimize performance giving the best chance for short-term survival.

In general, people react badly with either too little or too much stress in the long term. Without some sense of challenge (eustress or 'good' stress sensed as exhilaration and excitement), we would not get out of bed. In everyday normal stressful situations, the experience is pleasurable because one survives the threat.

In basic terms, stress is an aspect of living that can be beneficial when it motivates, inspires or encourages change. It can be the opposite when it does not (distress); individuals perceive that they do not have the resources to cope with a perceived situation from the past, present or future.

The 'stress' that people complain about is a feeling of tension or pressure experienced when demands placed upon them (stressors) are perceived as exceeding the resources they have available.

The stress cycle

The fight or flight response has been well researched and covered in earlier chapters. In terms of creating stress, it develops in the following cycle:

● The forebrain receives danger signals from eyes, ears and other senses and so on.

- The hypothalamus, in the brain, activates the pituitary gland to release hormones.
- Senses are activated, for example the pupils of the eyes dilate.
- Breathing rate increases and gets deeper.
- Heart rate and blood pressure increases.
- The liver releases sugar, cholesterol and fatty acids into the blood stream as fuel for fight or flight.
- Digestion ceases and bladder and bowel openings contract.
- The adrenal glands release hormones – adrenaline, noradrenaline and cortisone – which causes increased sweating and blood-clotting capacity.

The most common symptom is that people don't feel well and medical practitioners can find no clinical reason for it. However, as we covered in Sunday, during the Stone Age there would have been physical activity in fighting or running and the danger would have passed quickly.

Our innate primitive reactions

In the 21st century, the body response is the same but the threats we perceive are of a financial, emotional, mental and social nature. These types of threats are constantly present in our environment and are not generally dealt with quickly.

Stress-related illnesses

Being constantly stressed causes illness because the metabolic change is continuous, preventing relaxation or proper sleep for the body and the mind to repair itself. Some long-term effects can be: hair loss, headache, migraine, strokes, impaired immune response, nervousness, bad sleeping, neck and shoulder aches, lower back and leg ache, asthma, skin conditions, high blood pressure, bad circulation, heart diseases, some cancers, indigestion, ulcers, irritable bowel syndrome, impotency, menstrual disorders and rheumatoid arthritis. The negative effects of stress can also be visible in the form of bad decision-making, negative internal politics, reduced creativity and apathy.

If optimum performance is continually maintained or surpassed (chronic stress), then performance deteriorates rapidly and people eventually become ill or die. Chronic stress is a cumulative phenomenon that can develop over a lifetime or over a few weeks. A vicious circle or rather spiral is entered into with the stress response to fear driving an individual to produce more effort for less performance, with more time spent working and less time in relaxation.

Often it is not the obvious 'stress-straw' that 'breaks the camel's back'. In the working environment, chronic stress often develops from a lifestyle encouraged by employers to gain short-term competitive advantage, which has, say, a bereavement 'straw' or house move or relationship issue added to it. Absenteeism generated by chronic stress can cause a 'domino' collapse of employees as each person experiences overload when coping with their own work and that of an absent colleague.

Work–life balance

How well do you believe you balance your time between work and play and family and employer? As often happens, if there are feelings that the balance is not right, some typical reasons may be:

- You enjoy the work.
- You fear jeopardizing your career.
- You perceive that your boss expects it.

- You endure a workaholic organizational culture.
- You think that you have to prove you can cope.

Write up in your journal what you have discovered about your motivation for imbalances. Whatever the pressures on you at work, it is necessary to recognize the importance of relaxation and doing things that you enjoy.

Stress management strategies using EI

Because of the way a corporate EI programme is structured (this is covered on Thursday and Friday), it allows people to build the skills to reduce stress on a continual basis. Returning to the programme outcomes as a group every three months over a one-year period enables progress to be reviewed. Developmental areas can be shared and from this, creative solutions generated. Working with a group rewards the new behaviours being instilled.

Like risk, stress is a perception and therefore highly personal. Here is a series of checklists of stress management measures, which, by managing what we cannot avoid and by eliminating what we can, will lead to better health.

- Manage your relationships
- Manage your environment
- Manage your lifestyle
- Manage your attitude or reactions

Manage your relationships

- For one week, log notes in your journal about changes to your stress levels depending on who you are with at the time.
- Have authentic, emotionally intelligent relationships with people. Associate with those whose company you enjoy and who support you. Authenticity requires self-awareness and emotional expression so that when in conversation with an individual you are able to share your feelings openly, including any distractions impairing your ability to concentrate on them. The relationship would be equitable and based on a sense of mutuality. While the degree of give

and take may vary from time to time based on your needs, it would find an agreed equilibrium. When worries start to build up, talk to someone with whom you have a close relationship.

- Learn how to have assertive conversations with those who create anxiety by not acknowledging your feelings and rights. As much as possible, clear your life of people who drain your emotional battery creating unacceptable anxiety and conflict. Don't drift along in troublesome and distressing situations or relationships. Take action to change rather than trying to avoid the problem or deny it exists. Taking chances is the key to emotional well-being.
- Protect your personal freedoms and space. Do what you want and feel, but respect the rights of others. Don't tell others what to do, but if they intrude, let them know.
- Set up a co-coaching relationship with someone you trust, preferably someone with coaching experience. Meet at least once a month, split the time and have a scheduled phone call every week. Select life-improving books to read and share together. Tackle real issues including denial and avoidance with each other. Use your journal entries and prepare for the co-coaching sessions, writing the results up at the time and after reflection. Note the advice on coaching in Friday.
- Watch your conversations for faulty thought patterns, such as selective envy, disaster forecasting, finding the scapegoat, generalization and projecting our reactions onto others.

Having your battery drained

Manage your environment

- For one week, log in your journal notes changes to your stress levels and the environment you are in at the time.
- Being ruthless, identify the stressors and think what you can do about them (e.g. clutter in the house, shed and garage, or your journeys to work, or the lack of a study or 'den' for you).
- Surround yourself with cues from positive thoughts and relaxation.
- Find a time and place each day where you can have complete privacy. Take time off from others and pressures.

Manage your lifestyle

Change your lifestyle by removing the causes of stress. Look at the following:

- Effective time management is just one of many ways to keep from succumbing to stress overload.
- Make time to learn and practise relaxation or meditation skills.
- Engage in a vigorous physical exercise that is convenient and pleasurable. Check with your doctor before engaging on a new programme if you are unused to it. Sometimes it helps to get a friend to exercise with you to keep the discipline. Go to a gym or fitness centre that has instructors with recognized qualifications. Always do their induction session. Consider alternatives like learning to dance or join a club of some kind involving learning physical skills.
- Take short breaks during the day (every 45 minutes if working at a computer) which can help improve efficiency and well-being for the rest of the day. In addition, the breaks help with avoidance of problems with posture (lower back syndrome), eyesight and repetitive strain injuries (RSI).
- Maintain a reasonable diet and sane sleeping habits. Use alcohol in moderation and medication wisely, you must be in control of them and not vice versa. Avoid the use of sleeping pills, tranquillizers and other drugs to control stress. (Exercise really helps with sleeping problems as does a diet that acknowledges foods that can stimulate you throughout the day or encourage you to sleep at night.)

Manage your attitude

We are not upset by things but rather the view we take of them.
Epictetus

Consider whether you can have a positive attitude to something that is causing you and others around you to be under stress. It may be a weakness because of its extreme nature when it could be moderated and become a strength. Apart from the need to balance life and career, our personal characteristics play an important role in creating stress.

To see ourselves as others see us...

Seek the view of others on the characteristics that might add to your stress, such as:

- perfectionism
- misdirected anxiety
- need for approval of others
- pessimism
- impatience
- a wish to avoid conflict
- poor opinion of self.

If we wish to avoid undue stress, we must recognize the role such characteristics play and be prepared to modify our values. Reflect on this and write the results up in your journal.

Shortly, we will look at a stress audit that can start you on this programme as a diagnostic phase.

An EI approach to reducing stress

You might want to experiment to see what works best for you. The features of an emotionally intelligent approach that can tackle stress are:

- Increasing competencies in self-awareness, self-control and in awareness of others (empathy and appreciation).
- Viewing life as challenges to seek and not as obstacles to avoid. Review your obligations from time to time and make sure that they are still good for you. If they are not, let them go.
- Using assertiveness through a balance of responsive and assertive behaviours. Identifying positive approaches to events, rather than just tormenting yourself with negative thoughts and emotions.
- Understanding the true cost of our values and beliefs.
- Not becoming one-dimensional. Do not let one thing dominate you, such as a current project, schoolwork, relationships, career, sports, hobby and so on.
- Opening yourself to fresh experiences; try new-fangled things, novel foods and new places; take responsibility for your life and your feelings, but never blame yourself. Ownership of your life is a better philosophy than a blame culture.

Journal entries

Using the definitions of self-awareness and self-control, explore how EQ competencies can help you. Record thoughts in your journal after completion of the stress audit. This allows you to assess the impact of raising EQ on stress-reduction.

Reflection exercise

Pick out some competencies for self-control (from Tuesday) that you want to develop. Look at some strength that you want to use more. Think of routine events in the next two weeks that you can use to develop them. Set yourself some **smart** objectives (**s**pecific, **m**easurable, **a**ction-orientated, **r**ealistic and time-boxed). After two weeks, ask the following questions in self-study or with a friend or colleague.

● What was the single most challenging thing in the last two weeks about your behaviour change?
● What obstacles were there to stop you accomplishing your daily goals?
● Did the same distraction keep coming up or were the obstacles different each time?
● What helped you to succeed?
● What was the easiest thing for you in the last two weeks about your behaviour change?
● Did you know this insight about yourself before you began?
● Was there a time when you struggled with your goal? Record what day it was. What else was going on at the time?
● How did you bring yourself back into the 'here and now'? Can you do this at will?
● What was difficult about letting go of old behaviours – was there some pay-off in them for you? Did your internal observer talk to you and did you ignore the messages?

Write down the answers to the following questions:

● How do you see yourself at your best (e.g. if you are a perfectionist, you may be driving yourself too hard, striving for the impossible)?
● What, in the past 12 months, was the most challenging or exciting event in your life?
● In the past 12 months, what aspect of each event(s) was/ were most stressful?

Stress audit

Write down the answers to the following questions in your journal:

● Do you ever feel unable to cope?
● Do you find it difficult to relax?
● Do you ever feel anxious for no reason?
● Do you find it hard to show your true feelings?

- Are you finding it hard to make decisions?
- Are you often irritable for no reason?
- Do you worry about the future?
- Do you feel isolated and misunderstood?
- Do you doubt that you like yourself?
- Are you finding it difficult to concentrate?
- Do you find that life has lost its sparkle?
- I believe that for me stress is...
- Some stressors in my life are:
  - Life pressures
  - Satisfaction with life
  - General health and fitness
  - Quality of life
  - Relationships

Review previous journal entries to see what is related. Carry the learning on from one over to the other. You may find some barriers to learning or resistance to change.

Tomorrow we are taking EI development into the workplace for the whole organization.

Summary

Share the self-awareness, self-control and stress management content with a 'learning buddy' drawn from your personal or professional life. Discover the utility of it to you as an individual as well as a being a manager of others. Mutual respect and trust with no personal agenda is vital in sharing or eliciting insights with others.

You have covered:

● Stress identification & beneficial management strategies

● Stress definitions and the cycle of stress

● Stress-related illnesses with examples

● The consequences of not managing stress

● Work/life balance and your motivation to achieve it

● A stress audit and plan with management objectives

Agents of change need to model new behaviours. The exercises and recommended practices in this book will help you to be effective operating as a manager, helping to change your own organization.

Questions (answers at the back)

1. **The word stress is derived from which of the following?**
   a) An ancient English word for hardship or afflictions ❑
   b) Mechanical engineering ❑
   c) An archaic word for focus or emphasis ❑
   d) The Latin word *stringere*, which means to draw tight ❑

2. **Good stress is different and is known as...?**
   a) Eustress, which is experienced as exhilaration or excitement ❑
   b) Noradrenaline, which comes from the reptilian brain ❑
   c) Primary stress experienced in the amygdala ❑
   d) Cortisol, which soothes the brain ❑

3. **Select an answer that matches the assertion that 'No stress is good for you.'**
   a) True ❑
   b) False ❑
   c) False in some circumstances ❑
   d) Irrelevant, because there is no such state as no stress ❑

4. **The following are potential reactions to stress. Which ones reflect the chapter?**
   a) Senses are activated, pupils contract ❑
   b) Breathing rate increases and gets shallower ❑
   c) Heart rate and blood pressure decrease ❑
   d) The liver releases sugar, cholesterol and fatty acids into the bloodstream as fuel for fight or flight ❑

5. **Which one of the following is an incorrect reason why stress-related illnesses arise?**
   a) The metabolic change is continuous, preventing relaxation or proper sleep ❑
   b) Potential long-term effects are: hair loss, headache, migraine, strokes, impaired immune response, high blood pressure, bad circulation, heart diseases, some cancers, ulcers, irritable bowel syndrome ❑
   c) Effects of stress can be bad decision-making, internal politics, reduced creativity and apathy ❑
   d) Genetic predisposition to neurogenesis ❑

THURSDAY

Organizational change

Chapters up to now have covered the personal aspects of establishing your current levels of EI and deciding which strengths you want to develop as a priority. Today and Friday cover the organizational aspects of emotional intelligence such as how to create change, manage uncertainty and gain momentum. Part of the programme to do this should explore the answer to the question 'What will my company gain from an investment in EI?'. Most assessment providers are adept at helping prospective clients to define the business case and this chapter covers some economic considerations as a guide.

Today, we are going to gain an understanding of the following topics:

Investment in EI

The cost of low EQ

The positive effect of nurturing

How to create an EI culture

Journal entries

Investment in EI

Many people have a passion to reinvent their organization. I suggest here that creating an EI culture can be part of that reinvention. If you want to change the world, start by changing yourself.

> ### *You have to be the change you wish for the world.*
> (Mahatma Gandhi)

First, let us understand the business context by looking at a common scenario. In the 20th century, HR specialists sought to produce measures that:

- help the frontline to do anything faster, better, cheaper
- are clear enablers, neither barriers nor things that hamper operations.

You also have to generate differentiating products and services to get ahead of the competition and gain market share or lead the market.

However, I believe an EI culture can remove the friction that holds you back and can provide emotional stamina to tackle global challenges. According to Richard Hall, who writes about business creativity, when the Industrial Revolution began, we became engineers vesting in our left brain, which is interested in measurement, maths and 'minding the shop'. We probably need to move from the knowledge economy to an 'ideas economy', where both logical and creative capabilities are utilized to create innovations and to make them robust.

If the logical approach continues in recruiting people, we may be educating our brains in totally the wrong way for how the world really is now. Moreover, with the spread of social media, mobile devices and sophisticated applications at the fingertips, it may be totally the wrong way of development for how the world is going to develop. Staying the same in terms of what is valued, HR may be faced with leaders who hire people solely for knowledge and task-orientation, and not their emotional and social skills with customers, suppliers and colleagues. Does this sound familiar to you?

I believe that EI will define success in the 21st century, *doing* more will not be enough – *being* different might achieve higher goals.

Let us look at the economics of why we lose customers as well as staff for EQ-related reasons. In other words, we deliver superior products but the service aspect is lacking in some way. If you feel that your senior management will be disinclined to spend money on remedial work, you will need to develop an economic model to convince them.

It is 16 times cheaper to sell another product or service to an existing customer than to find a new customer. This applies to say, subscriptions services in the voluntary sector as much as commercial life (e.g. the RSPB is a bird conservation charity with a large membership who have an excellent online shop as well as outlets at many bird reserves).

It makes hard cash sense to expend effort in not only retaining existing satisfied customers but in converting them to advocates who recommend your products and services. Creating advocacy brings an average of five new customers at a very low cost of acquisition. You avoid outlay on direct mail, advertising, sales teams, and so on by reaching new customers in this way by word of mouth.

However, a dissatisfied customer will tell three times more people about you than an advocate does. Therefore, fifteen people will be put off using your product or service, which is very expensive.

How is this related to improvements in EQ? If the cause of complaint is skilfully explored, a transformation can be achieved. A customer can be converted to an advocate by skilful use of self-control, awareness and influencing skills. However, the emphasis should be on the beginning of the process and not potentially the end of their time as a customer.

Selecting people for their emotional and social capabilities and their match with the target customer base in order to focus on greater acquisition and less complaint handling has been seen to produce measurable results. (L'Oreal saw rises of 27 per cent in sales revenues through 'learned optimism' and selecting for EI capability in the case study mentioned in Sunday.)

The collection of high-quality and comprehensive information for marketing and R&D purposes also requires excellent social skills and awareness of others. In other words, the ability to build rapport and engender trust and to be in tune with the varying needs that customers have from a transaction with your organization. In a climate of trust, people can be open to cross sales from one product line to another or increasing the size of an order, known as upselling. In addition, if they feel treated well, information about major life events can be elicited, the type where big sums are involved: weddings, anniversaries, retirement planning, holidays and other family related referrals.

The cost of low EQ

Think back to Sunday and the three incidents involving a customer/supplier relationship or come up with other scenarios which apply.

- Think back to the exchanges between people.
- Estimate the costs involved in the outcome.
- Can you see that selecting people for their emotional and social capabilities and developing higher EQ can lead to sustainable, profitable relationships with customers and cheaper acquisition of new customers?
- Can you identify cost avoidance savings associated with a reduction in customer mishandling?
- What would all of the above look like on a spreadsheet analysis for your company? Is there a balance of advantage which justifies the investment?

You will need to develop an outline plan of each option for an organizational programme which can then have costs applied to establish whether there is a positive cost-benefit analysis and hence have the justification for implementation.

The positive effect of nurturing

Without compassionate and loving nurturing, an emergent adult may be without good work ethics, team working skills, communication capability and other skills at work to generate and contribute to economic success and to participate in a beneficial climate.

Professor Jim Fallon's statistically sound study of patterns in brain scans and blood tests (identifying a particular gene) have identified a population of psychopaths using blind trial data. The individuals displaying a specific pattern of brain dysfunction were in prison for murder, or were serial killers or displayed very violent antisocial behaviour. The data was mixed with those individuals with 'normal' scans and some with other clinical disorders or syndromes. However, the psychopathic profile was distinct and psychopathic people showed close correlations to each other. Further data was collected about their upbringing which strongly identified as common experience a neglectful childhood or one with violent parenting.

This association came much closer to home than Professor Fallon ever anticipated. Following a discussion of this study with his family, his mother suggested that he investigate a strand of the family living in the 19th century with 16 murders in their past. The family agreed to have both the tests done on them. Jim discovered that he had the (faulty) gene and the brain centre disposition which indicated the possibility of a psychopathic disposition.

Nevertheless, he had experienced a loving and happy childhood and the family were highly engaged with regular social interaction. However, everyone agreed that some traits were noticeable in terms of withdrawal at family events.

Jim believes that his good upbringing with careful nurturing meant that the psychopathic behaviours had never emerged in force. Remember what was said in Tuesday's chapter about the templates ingrained by the age of five in the amygdala (your autobiographical and emotional memory) leading to my assertion that skilled nurturing including praise is very important at the time and has much impact throughout adult life.

People are not naturally prone to giving positive feedback (Wheldall and Merrett). This varies from culture to culture and it may strike more or less of a note with you depending on your background. It may be the case that adults need to be educated to unlearn years of being covertly rewarded for cutting people down to size. Working in a culture that does not positively reinforce feedback becomes associated solely with negative comments. In this climate, praise is given in a vacuum of detail. However, criticism is remembered with 20/20 vision *forever*.

For praise to achieve its aim, there is a requirement to give specific evaluative feedback. This informs people about what they have done in particular, so that good behaviours become ingrained. However, due to fear of more accurate feedback being misconstrued as being unsupported criticism it is not unusual for managers to overplay the 'exceeds expectations' grading in performance appraisals. In this case, if accurate positive feedback is given, but it is not given rigorously and systematically, it is unlikely to result in changed behaviour. You may have to revisit the child within in order to engender a change in the adult by exploring:

- the climate in which they were brought up
- which behaviours were rewarded
- which behaviours were punished
- and how overtly or covertly this occurred.

The reasons why the practice of positive affirmation is a milestone in an emotionally intelligent culture are:

- It brings rewards, such as netting undiscovered potential, into the workplace.
- It allows teams to celebrate more and be positive with a regular sense of well-being.
- It avoids the language of human deficit that blocks cultures like cholesterol clogs arteries.

Positive affirmation does not have to be repeated many times to stick.

It can be combined with other techniques designed to take advantage of brain function and heightened emotional states.

Consider the previous assertion regarding the use of praise and positive assertion as a manager. How would it make you feel if your boss consistently treated you this way? Come up with ideas on how to practise positive affirmation as a manager yourself. Record in your journal your reaction to your answers and any thoughts regarding them.

How to create an EI culture

In this and the next chapter, we are going to explore how to create an EI culture.

El culture change project life cycle

A typical life cycle for an El culture change project has the following stages (run in parallel to some degree using different resources):

Stage 1: Creating the El team
Stage 2: Diagnosing and exploring change
Stage 3: Closure of issues surrounding the old culture and discovering the new culture
Stage 4: Two-way communication of the dream or vision for the new culture
Stage 5: Designing a programme to deliver the dream or vision, including what has to be given up
Stage 6: Piloting the design pragmatically
Stage 7: Reviewing the pilot and matching the results against expectations
Stage 8: Completing the cycle for the rest of the organization
Stage 9: Activities and practices sustaining the results

Stage 1: Creating the El team

With businesses under pressure financially and competitively, it is not a good idea to utilize consultants on repeated activities that could be done by internal or specialist staff after they have been given extra capabilities. To be economic, a 'forest fire' approach is expedient (starts from a point selected by external experts and is spread outwards by a handpicked internal El team). The El team is composed of those with good facilitation skills and an affiliative approach, selected from your available resources:

● the Organizational Development team
● HR or Training and Development teams
● volunteers – highly engaged at work, inspiring individuals dedicated to reinventing the organization (but take care to check how you are going to select volunteers for their suitability)
● external specialists hired for their expertise in transformation and their ability to transfer knowledge and skills by training and coaching the internal El team.

The EI team members may need to go through a formal assessment process to get the mix right for the programme, which includes as far as possible a 360-degree emotional intelligence assessment. The skills of these individuals could be raised by a number of interventions: coaching and assessment, paired facilitation of others, regular feedback and continuous professional development (CPD).

If available funding is extremely low, a bespoke 'Train the EI coach' course can be developed and delivered by the HR Manager (or project sponsor if that role is going to be very hands-on). This course should include how to evaluate the potential of the EI team back in their new role.

Developed to become resilient EI change agents and coaches, members must be able to cope well with participants enduring the agonies of raising themselves through the learning ladder (see Sunday). During workshop sessions, specific change issues will impact participants' lives. They will be confronted by what it means for them to meet the new demands of the business.

Rolling it out as a pilot programme, the EI team would transfer change agency to managers and staff as quickly as possible with expert guidance as required.

After creating the EI team, I recommend that you begin with a diagnostic phase in order to understand the current organizational culture. This provides an opportunity to finalize the way forward.

Stage 2: Diagnosing and exploring change in your organization

Run through the following checklist thinking about your current organization. Which of them can you tick without any doubts in your mind?

Organizational checklist

❑ My organization has a strategic view.
❑ Senior people energize others lower in the system.
❑ Leaders here create a structure that follows function.
❑ Managers make decisions at a point when the relevant information is held or comes together.

❏ This company has a reward system that balances what you know and what you do.
❏ We have relatively open communication.
❏ We reward collaboration when it is in the organization's best interests.
❏ Our managers manage conflict, they do not suppress it.
❏ Our leaders view the organization as an open system and manage the demands put upon it.
❏ Our organization values individuality and individuals.
❏ We actively learn through feedback.

The organizational checklist is part of a Healthy Organization Checklist by Beckhard in his work *Organizational Transitions – Managing Complex Change*. The more ticks indicates the greater health of your organization. Review this alongside the description of a positive organizational climate (the work based on George Litwin and Robert Stringer referred to in Monday). Record in your journal your reaction to each answer and any thoughts regarding reinvention. You could consider the organizational checklist to be a series of milestones for entry into a change management plan for the EI culture change project. This could include management development to assist managers generate healthy leadership styles that contribute to a positive climate at work.

If you have ticked all of Beckhard's list, then you are fortunate to work in an organization that is emotionally literate and shares learning. I recommend that you share the checklist with as many people as possible to come up with a joint diagnosis. You will be unable to mobilize people to change without such agreement.

Diagnosing change
● Thinking about change in your organization, what kind of change do you want in the following areas?
  – Organizational policies
  – Leadership styles
  – Environment
  – Relationships
  – Processes, procedures or practices
  – Attitudes
  – Behaviour

- For each of the above, who needs to be involved?
- How ready or fit for change is your organization?
- How prepared is it for the changes you want?
- Who or what are the forces for and against the changes?
- How realistic are the changes you want?
- How can you modify your change needs to make them more realistic?
- What resources can you tap into?
  - Help from Government, such as grants, cheap loans, agencies and business schemes?
  - Central resources as part of a group or larger organization?
  - Internal teams set up for this purpose?
  - Volunteers? How will you measure their suitability?
- Thinking of your organization at present:
  - Which part is most vulnerable to change from external drivers?
  - Which part is most vulnerable to change from internal drivers?

Record the answers in your journal. If you do not know the answers, then enquire into how a change process might be initiated in your organization. People often feel safer doing some exploration about what change would feel like and how it could happen. See Stage 3 as mandatory if you are in this situation.

Stage 3: Closure of issues

For the want of a stage like this, many culture change programmes fail to achieve a critical mass of transformation. To generate an EI culture, it is vital for staff to let go of allegiance to the previous culture. There may be a good deal to give up in the way of unproductive behaviours, to which work-based teams are attached (albeit unknowingly). You need to discover what values people are wedded to on a daily basis and how these compare with any new values.

If they sense that you view the old culture as wrong and the reason for moving forward is to put things right, this does not give credit for what has worked. Many people may have taken to heart a previous mission, vision and values. Start with praise of what has been achieved to date to show respect, and to translate the success to the new paradigm collaboratively through skilled facilitation. In addition, it is vital that the reward and remuneration mechanisms are updated to incentivize the new behaviours. Therefore, recognition of achievements is a vital part of Stage 3 completion and people's ability to buy-in to the new.

Common business scenarios are of mergers or acquisitions where programmes are initiated in the shadow of earlier ones. People may feel that previous work goes unrecognized, and this may stop them supporting the new ideas and methods. They may not even be aware of previous beliefs and actions; it is possible for cultures to be implicit rather than explicit.

In order for staff to alter both attitudes and behaviour, they need to understand 'What's in it for me'. Research shows that without this understanding people may *appear* to change without fundamentally altering their attitudes or behaviour.

It is safer for them to stay where they are in terms of mindset, not to buy in or even for people to sabotage the new culture. There is always a pay-off for behaving in these ways, such as:

- getting to be right
- playing the cynic and never having to commit to anything
- dominating or bullying others
- self-justification
- blaming others and not being responsible
- martyrdom – professional victims frequently switch places and persecute their victimizer.

What is needed is to be clear about the present culture, lay it to rest, and model the new. Without this, fundamental step change will not occur.

Regenerate enthusiasm for the organization moving onto the next stage by checking the sense of 'permission to proceed'. The permission status may be manifest in hard management decisions on financial approvals for change consultancy or for staff being released from operations for change events.

It is essentially a contracting issue for the EI team whose mission it is to change the organization with those who officially (and unofficially) hold sway in the organization. We'll continue these stages tomorrow.

Journal entries

Study the following actions to ensure success and make notes in your journal on how they apply to your organization.

Actions to ensure success

- Make sure that employees are clear about the previous culture.
- Celebrate past achievements; provide opportunities for them to feel acknowledged for what they've done well.
- Avoid any elitism of the Executive having higher-paid coaches than the workforce.

Summary

Today, we have examined the creation of the EI team responsible for change agency. We have determined the need for closure on past ways and respect for what has been achieved. Tomorrow, we move on to look at implementation.

Practical advice is given stage by stage and for different situations such as low resources, skills or funding:

● Diagnosing and exploring change in your organization to manage uncertainty and gain momentum
● Looking at the economics of creating very satisfied customers and advocates willing to recommend your products or company
● Exploring the costs of poor outcomes resulting from low emotional intelligence being applied in a situation
● Examining the positive effect of nurturing as a strategy to encourage others and to ingrain good behaviours
● Exploring the first three stages of an emotionally intelligent culture change programme:

1 Creating the change team
2 Diagnosing and exploring the implications of change
3 Closure of long-standing issues before moving on to implement necessary changes

Questions (answers at the back)

1. **Which of the following identifies the number of new customers an advocate might bring through recommendation?**
   a) 15 ❏
   b) 4 ❏
   c) 16 ❏
   d) 5 ❏

2. **How many prospective customers might a complainant put off coming to you?**
   a) 5 ❏
   b) 15 ❏
   c) 16 ❏
   d) 4 ❏

3. **How much cheaper is it to sell another product or service to an existing customer than to find a new customer?**
   a) 15 times ❏
   b) 16 times ❏
   c) 5 times ❏
   d) 4 times ❏

4. **Which costs are avoided or reduced by advocacy?**
   a) Direct mail ❏
   b) Advertising ❏
   c) Sales teams ❏
   d) All of the above and more ❏

5. **Select the type of analysis suggested to develop justification for an EQ programme.**
   a) Spreadsheet analysis ❏
   b) Cost-benefit analysis ❏
   c) Balance of advantage ❏
   d) An outline plan with costs of each option ❏

6. **Which of the following attributes contribute to economic success and aid in a beneficial climate at work?**
   a) Good work ethics ❏
   b) Team working skills ❏
   c) Communication capability ❏
   d) Attitude to bad habits ❏

7. **Which of the following is an incorrect description of an advantage which good nurturing and praise can bring?**
   a) It allows teams to celebrate more and be positive with a regular sense of well-being ❏
   b) It brings rewards, such as netting larger bonuses ❏
   c) Praise does not have to be repeated often to stick ❏
   d) It can be combined with other techniques designed to take advantage of brain function and heightened emotional states ❏

FRIDAY

Designing a change programme

This chapter continues the theme of you as a manager taking a role in transforming the organization. It continues from Stages 1–3 in Thursday, and now focusses on communications strategies and designing a pilot programme, covering the following issue:

How to create an EI culture

How to create an EI culture

Continuing from Thursday, today we are going to explore how to create an EI culture, starting with the following diagrams.

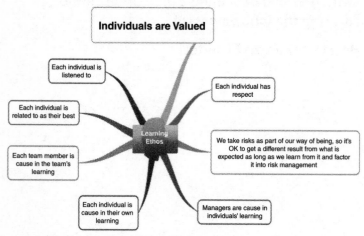

Individuals are Valued

Each individual is listened to

Each individual is related to as their best

Each team member is cause in the team's learning

Each individual is cause in their own learning

Learning Ethos

Each individual has respect

We take risks as part of our way of being, so it's OK to get a different result from what is expected as long as we learn from it and factor it into risk management

Managers are cause in individuals' learning

Developed by Dr. Cathie Woodward BA (Hons) BPhil MA with Jill Dann

With a presiding ethos that individuals are valued:

- Each individual has respect from others, for themselves and for the team.
- Each individual is actively listened to.
- Each individual is related to as they are at their best.
- Each team member has responsibility for and encouragement to contribute to the learning of everyone in the team and collectively as a group.
- Each team member has responsibility for their own learning and is encouraged to learn more about their own learning preferences, best learning experiences and ability to self-direct their progression.
- Every manager has responsibility for and encouragement to contribute to the learning of everyone in the team, and collectively as a group, sharing his/her own learning.

As part of our way of being, we take risks expanding our possibilities and opportunities. It is OK to take risks. If we get an unexpected result different to expectations, this is OK as long as we learn from it and incorporate everything we have learned including our risk log and management.

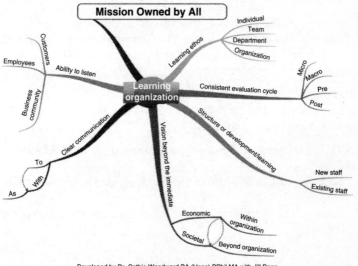

Developed by Dr. Cathie Woodward BA (Hons) BPhil MA with Jill Dann

The learning environment is one that embodies:

- a mission owned by all and a learning ethos as previously described
- an organization designed to listen to its business community, employees and customers and acknowledge feedback
- processes, practices and policies designed to facilitate clear communication
- a vision that stretches beyond the immediate economic and societal boundaries within and beyond the organization
- a structure of development and learning for new and existing staff that is a continuum following the employee life cycle and aligned with the learning ethos

- an evaluation cycle consistent at the macroscopic level and the microscopic level covering pre- and post-learning interventions
- a learning environment that facilitates an 'ideas economy' seeking collaboration, partnerships, third-party added-value providers, academic partners and the sharing of knowledge and emotional capital as far as is feasible.

I believe that the EI programme can go a long way towards achieving the advantages of being a learning organization. In your journal, taking a clockwise scan around each of the mind maps, do some reflection on:

- where your organization is at present
- where it wants to be in the future and by when
- how it might get there.

What are the implications for you as a manager of people and the change process?

Does it look like a roadmap for a strategy and implementation programme?

What needs to be further explored or fleshed out to complete a roadmap?

Stage 4: Two-way communication

The communication of the dream or vision for the new EI culture must be effective in both ways, reporting from top to bottom and vice versa:

- The strategy must enrol all staff in the new approach clearly stating the benefits, including financial ones, and speculative risks.
- The strategy must ensure that there is sponsorship of the new culture by those with power in the organization.

Actively increase 'shop floor' participation using skills transferred from change agents. Plan to reduce over time the scale of intervention by change agents, managers, consultants or trainers. Do not reduce the effort for continuous professional development (CPD), education or communication.

It is often economic to bring in experienced executives who can model the new behaviours and it is not unusual for senior executives who cannot to elect to leave.

Stage 5: Designing a programme

A culture change project should start with a self-awareness programme (Step 1 below). If members of staff are not able to see themselves as others see them, it is pointless attempting to raise their social skills and awareness of others. The design must include what has to be given up to achieve the dream or vision.

The five-step EI team programme

To create the EI team, I recommend a five-step training and development process laid out below. Training means running two-day events as described in Steps 1–5 below taken over a minimum of six months to a year. The coaching phases are between these events to embed learning. I would suggest that a pivotal goal is that the EI team creates a 'critical mass' of advocates and exemplars of the new culture. It is essential that this programme be considered a business priority. The whole company should be put through as many of the steps as can be afforded with a recommended minimum of the two marked with an asterisk.

Step 1: ***Foundation** (see Monday): Self-awareness and knowledge about own EI competencies – awareness of feelings, personal insight and self-assurance. Identification of a first set of unproductive behaviours and commitment to change through development back in the workplace.

Step 2: ***Generating an internal observer** (see Tuesday): Using increased self-awareness from Step 1 to increase self-control by identifying the emotional triggers to unproductive behaviour – enhancing self-regulation, authenticity, accountability, flexibility and self-motivation.

Step 3: **Change agency and stress management** (see Wednesday): Using Steps 1 and 2 to understand sources of stress, to generate and commit to stress management strategies. Understanding and utilizing change management techniques suitable for self, use with others and organizationally.

Step 4: **Conflict management, negotiation and assertive behaviour:** Influencing strategies and techniques are explored to resolve conflict equitably, to reconcile differences in negotiations and to practise assertive behaviour.

Step 5: **Developing specific EI coaching skills:** Using a seven-phase coaching process as illustrated below. (For more detail and method see Cook, Marshall J. *Effective Coaching*, McGraw-Hill 2011.)

5.1 **Contracting phase** – The challenge faced by the individual and the required outcome are identified. The contract for the coaching relationship is explored and the commitment is made.

5.2 **The coaching approach** – Possible approaches to the coaching process are brainstormed based on understanding of the context of the challenge as well as the employees' personal issues. Lateral thinking is encouraged and unconventional ideas given consideration.

5.3 **The action plan** – The first meeting needs to complete some time management and the practical aspects of the coaching environment. What type of environment is suitable to the nature of the challenge (complete privacy needed or relative privacy of noisy public venue)? What aids might be needed if any?

5.4 **Agree deadlines** – What is the schedule and arrangements for changing it (revisit contract if required)?

5.5 **Evaluation** – What are the criteria for evaluation of success? How will the coachee know when the coaching is working? When will the coach establish that his or her subject is not coachable on this topic?

5.6 **Facilitate action** – What can you as coach do to help your employees succeed? Facilitation involves avoiding being tempted to rescue employees, thus stealing their autonomy of action and thought. Paternalistic or maternalistic approaches that take over the task from the employee are diametrically opposed to the learning ethos.

5.7 **Follow through** – This is a collaborative way of enforcing deadlines and setting time to review progress to ensure that well-intentioned plans do not get lost.

Working with the executive layer, the programme may be cyclical with the first batch becoming 'super coaches'. Coherent management of the change programme can be achieved by merging EI competencies with hard managerial and analytical skills.

EI learning methodology

The programme should generate opportunities for experiential learning, sharing knowledge of EI and change agency. Permanent processes, systems and practices should be instilled using the experience gained and following the accepted learning ethos.

Classroom-based work

By being very interactive, participants practise the skills they are developing through a variety of training methods, which meet delegates' varying learning styles:

- a variety of accelerated learning techniques and exercises to help practise new skills and knowledge
- mind mapping to speed learning and ensure a thorough understanding of the new concepts
- presentation and discussion of relevant material and debate to facilitate understanding of their role in the organization

- self/peer evaluated role-plays to allow delegates to practise skills and to facilitate self-assessment of their own developing skills
- activities allowing delegates to understand themselves and the ways they interact with others, for example games to understand how they relate to colleagues and customers (both internal and external), or team building exercises to facilitate support of each other in their new roles.

Development at work

Working with the business to embed EI coaching in the culture and processes, developmental learning back at work should be provided to ensure success within the work context. Exercises should be designed to fit in with routine events in the workplace, for example team meetings. This will include the following:

- focus groups, webinars or workshops, for example ways of developing structures to generate the EI programme internally
- directed self-study and shared EI exercises
- learning sets and cross-functional teams including partners where appropriate
- e-learning to share knowledge and experience (i.e. if you have the technology and are globally disparate)
- one-to-one coaching or supervised/observed coaching sessions or team coaching.

Learning outcomes for EI culture change interventions

People behave as they are rewarded. Organizations waste money by charging ahead with training while delaying alignment of reward mechanisms to the learning outcomes.

This is essential in Stage 5. Mismatches are very disillusioning for participants. Once you know what hard performance indicators and behavioural competencies are required, you must act on this.

In order for participants to continue to adopt a positive approach throughout the organization, it is important that they have coaching immediately following each course. It would be helpful if their consolidation successes are recognized (rewards, reviews, appraisal, etc.).

Learning outcomes of the five-step programme

By the end of the programme, the EI team will have achieved all the learning outcomes:

● Have a sense of self-esteem and self-confidence and the ability to maintain them under all circumstances – successfully managing themselves in challenging situations

● Further develop a variety of interpersonal skills, for example assertiveness, managing their own emotional responses, rapport building

● Display integrity, honesty and authenticity, when dealing with colleagues, creating more effective teams

● Be able to recognize when they relate to people using their previous opinions rather than looking for opportunities to reinforce new behaviours

● Have measured their approach to feedback and discussed the present organizational culture

● Understand how to use positive feedback in order to change behaviour

● Improve their strategies to consistently generate positive feedback

● Be able to self-assess their positive feedback to employees

● Understand the purpose of EI coaching and be able to analyse their strengths and areas of development as coaches

● Respect the autonomy of action and thought of people they coach

Stage 6: Piloting the design pragmatically

Do not select the worst region because you want to change it the most and think that this will form a useful pilot. Your consultant team may well be experienced enough to tackle this region but your new EI coaches may find it too big a step. This will be demoralizing and you need to start with a winner. In surrounding regions that have taken the transformation well and have emotional stamina, you can always restructure (each absorbing parts of the difficult region) using the critical mass.

Make sure that you have consulted all stakeholders on the pilot evaluation criteria. Be clear that you know what good looks like in the new behavioural competencies in the opinion of all the key decision-makers. To sustain the new culture, it is essential that those who will judge competence are reliable and consistent.

Usually consultants 'start the fire' and teach others how to spread it with a wedge of resources that reduces with time. The goal is for the EI team to transfer all of their knowledge and skills to the business through experiential learning. The approach will only be successful if the recipients pick up all of the skills needed from the consultants and do not dilute the messages.

It is wise for the EI team to remain ahead of the learning curve to maintain a gap between them and the main body of personnel. They are then able to support staff stopping any cultural shear between workers, supervisors, middle managers and the executive level.

During the transition phase, EI team members would have coaching supervision (i.e., be coached) to ensure that they have understood the models, practice and experience of EI coaching. The transition phase would be to complete the transfer of knowledge. Evaluation would be a continuous process, thereby ensuring that business needs are met.

The pilot would then be used to decide to what scale external support remains necessary and to complete the implementation plan for the wider organization based on success. Costs, benefits and the balance between them can be fleshed out using the evidence collected as well as any other anecdotal evidence such as feedback from clients, suppliers and those impacted elsewhere in the organization.

Stage 7: Reviewing the pilot

Reviewing the pilot and matching the results against expectations, I would not expect to see financial payback in less than 12 months. However, within three months, I would expect individuals to evidence and report personal perceptions of benefit. They may be able to quote specific examples where use of their new EI competencies generated new business, protected existing business, increased sales, or increased advocacy, for example handling customer complaints.

Stage 8: Completing the cycle

Completing the cycle for the rest of the organization is vital. However, there are too many variables to give detailed advice here other than some general guidelines.

● Have a communications strategy right from the start that uses formal and informal chains of communication.
● Plan the change programme professionally, paying equal attention to the psychological process that people will go through, as you do to the tasks, goals and techniques employed. (For example, see the work of Elisabeth Kübler-Ross regarding how change is processed.)
● Ideally, everyone in the company should receive at least the first two courses, which concentrate on achieving heightened self-awareness and a capability to use this awareness to increase self-control. Each of these should then be followed by a period of development back in the workplace.

- Put first-line supervisors through the programme first if you have to limit the volume. You will have to make a judgement using your knowledge of the current culture and management styles that prevail. Potentially, you can afford to leave middle management until quite late but not executives, specialists or first-line supervisors as they generate more risk if they are living the old culture. However, everyone must be part of the two-way communication strategy so no one feels left out and everyone understands the reasons for the manner in which interventions are scheduled.

- Have a feedback loop that evaluates comments from participants carefully, remembering where they are on the learning ladder. Participants can kick out at trainers and change agents when the subject matter is confronting because it is below their level of self-awareness (they do not know what they do not know). Anticipate this and have change techniques to hand, being prepared to give individuals extra coaching (refer back to the five-step course for the EI team). You must also have ensured that they go back from the course into a climate that is supporting the transformation by preparing and briefing those concerned. Communication is key to embedding the development back in the workplace.

- Do not be surprised if strong bonds emerge between the EI coaches and participants on their courses. Collaborative approaches between first-line supervisors and the EI team will make the transition back to work seamless. Make the transition work by a process of encouraging supervisors to coach people emerging from courses, and by the EI team coaching the supervisors.

- Complete risk management exercises at three levels: business (speculative or good risks where you are speculating to accumulate), programme level (where many projects interact and are dependent) and the individual project level where they vary depending on the nature (information system, building move, training life cycle).

- Key influencers and leaders in the business must reinforce the new culture. Methods of continuing the development of the organization were included in the learning methodology in Stage 5.

Competency assessment

By adopting a coaching style of leadership, managers both motivate employees to work harder and generate a more positive culture. This also facilitates retention of key staff. Using competency assessment techniques will support continuous improvement of operations:

● discriminating competencies – that separate superior performers from average performers
● core competencies – characteristics that a sample of people in a job would have in common and those that are needed to get the basic job done.

The coach can spread discriminating competencies from one individual (say high cross-sales results due to excellent questioning skills) across the team.

Thus over time, yesterday's core competencies evolve based on the observed discriminating competencies of today.

New joiners will be selected on the basis of the higher standard as previous discriminating competencies become labelled as core because the bar is being continuously raised.

The overall standard of the team rises with time, based on this learning cycle of continuous improvement.

Stage 9: Sustaining the results

Maintaining the change through a coaching culture and creating a strategy for the learning organization/environment is important.

Develop a range of programme outcomes that you would like to achieve and incorporate these into a plan. You will want to have any survey material of requirements or opinions/feedback to hand and ideas on how to instil the right ethos and principles to make the change enduring.

● Learning ethos
● Structure or development/learning
● Learning environment
● Governance

Summary

As a manager taking a role in transforming the organization, you should now have sufficient information to work with internal teams and consultants on your own programme. Tomorrow, we develop a Personal Development Plan based on what we have learned.

You have now covered:

- Designing a new emotionally-literate culture
- Stage 4: Generating two-way communication for the new culture
- Stage 5: Designing the 5-step change programme to deliver the dream or vision
- Stage 6: Piloting the design of the change programme pragmatically
- Stage 7: Reviewing the pilot data matching the results against expectations to retune the programme
- Stage 8: Completing the cycle , rolling it out to all company areas and clearing up the pilot region
- Stage 9: Activities and practices sustaining the results. Maintaining the change through a coaching culture

Questions (answers at the back)

1. **Which of the following correctly align with the learning ethos described in the chapter?**
   a) Each individual is related to as they are at their best ☐
   b) A team member will be appointed who has responsibility for and encouragement to contribute to the learning of everyone in the team and collectively as a group ☐
   c) Each team member has responsibility for following their manager's development plan for them ☐
   d) Every manager has responsibility for the learning of everyone in the team, sharing his or her own learning ☐

2. **Which of the following align with the learning environment described in the chapter?**
   a) The organization is designed to tell its business community, employees and customers what it is planning ☐
   b) Its processes, practices and policies are designed to facilitate clear communication ☐
   c) The vision stretches beyond the immediate building boundaries ☐
   d) The structure of development and learning for new and existing staff is a continuum following the employee life cycle and aligned with the learning ethos ☐

3. **Which of the following reflects guidance on two-way communication?**
   a) The communication of the dream or vision for the new EI culture must be effective both ways, reporting from top to bottom and vice versa ☐
   b) The strategy must enrol all staff in the new approach clearly stating the benefits, including financial ones, and speculative risks ☐
   c) The strategy must ensure that there is sponsorship of the new culture by those with power in the organization ☐
   d) Actively increase 'shop floor' participation using skills transferred from change agents ☐

4. **Which one of the following is an incorrect reflection of the 5-step EI team programme?**
   a) Self-awareness and knowledge about own EI competencies ☐
   b) Generating an internal observer – self-control and emotional literacy ☐
   c) Change agency and appointment of a stress manager ☐
   d) Conflict management, negotiation and assertive behaviour ☐

5. **The following reflect sequential phases for coaching of the EI team between events. Which one is out of sequence?**
   a) Contracting phase ☐
   b) Coaching approach ☐
   c) The action plan ☐
   d) Evaluation criteria ☐

SATURDAY

Successful self-directed learning

We have come full circle now, back from looking at ourselves as individuals and our interactions with others through to how we create an entire organization that is emotionally intelligent and with a healthy learning environment for all. We arrive back, looking at ourselves from both a personal point of view and as one who operates in an organization or management role with others. Today, you will design your own programme for intentional change, looking at:

The employee life cycle

Preparing for the next developmental steps

The employee life cycle

Organizations rely on staff for the revenue for the business. The chart shows a central flow of processes during their time as an employee – from recruitment through deployment and their exit strategy.

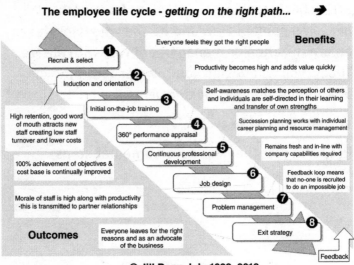

The employee life cycle - *getting on the right path...* ➡

① Recruit & select	Everyone feels they got the right people **Benefits**
② Induction and orientation	Productivity becomes high and adds value quickly
③ Initial on-the-job training	Self-awareness matches the perception of others and individuals are self-directed in their learning and transfer of own strengths

High retention, good word of mouth attracts new staff creating low staff turnover and lower costs

④ 360° performance appraisal — Succession planning works with individual career planning and resource management

⑤ Continuous professional development — Remains fresh and in-line with company capabilities required

100% achievement of objectives & cost base is continually improved

⑥ Job design — Feedback loop means that no-one is recruited to do an impossible job

Morale of staff is high along with productivity -this is transmitted to partner relationships

⑦ Problem management

Outcomes — Everyone leaves for the right reasons and as an advocate of the business

⑧ Exit strategy

Feedback

© Jill Dann July 1992–2012

The benefits of a closed-loop process such as this are as follows:

- Everyone feels they got the right people in post.
- Productivity becomes high and adds value quickly.
- High retention, good word of mouth attracts new staff.
- There is low turnover of staff.
- There are low costs.
- Self-awareness matches the perception of others and individuals are self-directed in their learning and transfer of own strengths.
- Succession planning works with individual career planning and resource management.
- 100 per cent achievement of objectives and cost base is continually improved.

- Employee capability remains fresh and in line with required company capabilities.
- Feedback loop means that no one is recruited to do an impossible job.
- Morale of staff is high along with productivity – this is transmitted to partner relationships.
- Everyone leaves for the right reasons and as an advocate of the business and its brands.

Conversely, should managers be unable to complete these steps, then symptoms and problems may arise as follows:

- Morale and motivation are often blamed when it is simply a matter of incomplete processes or a lack of comprehensive policies or leadership issues falling between the steps.
- Early negative attitudes mean that people leave prematurely.
- Low productivity, high number of accidents and absenteeism start to occur.
- Low morale of staff leaks to customer relationships.
- Bottom line results are poor and cost base is high.
- Short-term strategy is expensive if the feedback loop is left open – for example if no exit interviews are undertaken to inform other processes.

Thinking more in the shoes of the employee needs to be measured against strategic goals and new value-based behaviours, e.g. what achieves profitability sustainably.

Preparing for the next developmental steps

We are now going to explore what you might do after completing this book, by gaining an understanding of the following topics:

- The value of keeping a journal
- What a Personal Development Plan is and why it is useful
- Guidelines for completing a professional development analysis
- Designing a programme for you
- Steps in development

The value of keeping a journal

On Sunday, we covered the format for a journal entry and some experience concerning the value of doing so. The idea of keeping a journal is to consistently log your learning, keeping the information in one place readily to hand (possibly on a Smartphone or tablet), and thus making it as easy as possible to do this. Alternatively, use the following formats and keep the logs in your Personal Development Plan folder:

● Learning log questionnaire
● Emotional intelligence exercise log

Learning log questionnaire

Give details of your role at that time and whether you are being supervised in these activities. Then record answers to the following bullets:

● Learning goals being worked on
● Record of the last exercise completed
● What learning occurred?
● List your main strengths and weaknesses during the exercise.
● What learning goals do you wish to continue working on?
● Other comments

Emotional intelligence exercise log

Create a simple four-column table. Leave whole rows between the exercises, so that you can repeat each exercise with different people.

Exercise number	Date completed	With whom	Remarks

You need to record the self-observations and reports from others accurately as you develop using these exercises and guidance.

What a Personal Development Plan is and why it is useful

A Personal Development Plan (PDP) should start with a baseline entry developed using some techniques, such as a professional development analysis. Guidelines are given for this below. The PDP should be maintained throughout training. If possible, it can be updated every day using the learning outcomes, session objectives or teaching points as a structure. Personal development progress should be judged against agreed criteria for every job. Any gaps identified can be developed through a variety of methods, such as coaching and formal learning events. The choices available have been described earlier in the week.

If your organization conducts 360-degree appraisals feeding into your PDP, try to keep the identification of gaps in a positive framework. If it becomes known that this process is always used to elicit weaknesses that are used in performance-related pay, then the shared insights will become defensive in nature. This will prevent a healthy learning pattern forming.

Guidelines for completing a professional development analysis

SWOT

To start a professional development analysis, you need to complete a SWOT (strengths/weaknesses/opportunities/threats) table of four quadrants that considers:

- Internal – strengths and weaknesses: Consider these in specialist, technical and business skills and personal effectiveness (your EI competencies).
- External – opportunities and threats: Consider the impact of environmental drivers and personal factors including lifestyle plans.

You might like to consider those areas of weakness important to the business or to you personally. Similarly in respect of your strengths, there may be a business opportunity that requires you to develop one or more of these further, that is, to expert level. Strengths and weaknesses must be considered in the light of the opportunities and threats.

Competency analysis

This involves identifying those capabilities required for a job or future aspiration. Identify the skills, knowledge and experience that are required to successfully meet the current and future requirements of your role and record them in a table such as this:

Competency analysis table				
Skills, knowledge and experience required for job or future aspirations	Important/ urgent	Current level 1–5	Target level 1–5	Gap description and size

Important/urgent grading

Score each skill according to its importance and urgency.

Recognize what motivates you and expect it to have a higher priority. However, you may decide that a skill is less important but as part of personal growth you still wish to give it a high priority.

In addition to the above imperatives, identify those skills you might like to develop that will enrich or broaden you professionally and personally.

Competency – current level and target level

Grade your current level of competency on a scale of 1–5 and then define the target level that you would like to achieve:

1 (Expert) – practising at a level of excellence with high degree of skill and vast knowledge base
2 (Practitioner) – proficient and above minimum standard required due to experience and advanced knowledge
3 (Foundation) – meets minimum standard of competence, familiar and able to use relevant knowledge and skill
4 (Basic) – some or little knowledge/skill, but unable to practise at a competent level
5 (Novice) – no knowledge/skill, requires extensive training

Gap analysis

Having identified your current and target level of competence, calculate the difference between the two levels.

This figure will help you form a basis to identify those aspects that require professional development.

Having completed the SWOT and competency analyses, consider those skills areas requiring development, taking into consideration:

● the scale of gap based on the analysis of your skills, experience and knowledge
● how important, urgent or critical they are to your current role or future aspirations.

Break down any large gaps into stages to make them manageable. Be realistic and identify what is achievable to be motivating. Consider further self-appraisal and feedback from clients, colleagues, mentors and others on your behaviour and emotional knowledge.

Designing a programme for you

To design a programme for you, you need to understand your learning preferences and prejudices. Skills and knowledge are usually acquired through training interventions away from work and on-the-job training. In addition, you can ask to be given real organizational issues to tackle as projects to acquire experience and broaden your development. Development options include self-study, learning sets, cross-functional teams, and through use of learning technologies.

From Sunday's work, you will appreciate that raising EQ is possible because EI is learnable. Complete a learning styles assessment to determine your tendencies. (Try either www. peterhoney.com for his Learning Series or www.haygroup.com for Hay McBer, whose learning styles inventory can align with leadership styles and an ECI 360 assessment.)

Expect to have two learning styles that predominate but you are not stuck with the two alone. If you can undertake development activity to round off your learning styles to include all four behavioural patterns, this improves your problem-solving and solutions, teamwork and communication capability. This means that you are processing information and learning most comprehensively and understand those with preferences different to your own. It will save you a lot of time in the medium to long term.

Employee life cycle chart

Following the employee life cycle illustrated at the start of this chapter, which illustrates the benefits of joined-up processes, consider any symptoms of mismatches and unwanted outcomes. You should start your PDP on joining your first organization. Update it at every life cycle step for the rest of your career. Examples of PDP entries:

1 Induction and initial business training
2 On-the-job rehearsal
3 Coaching sessions
4 Continuous learning through continuous professional development (CPD), including structures for developing further line responsibility by embedding reward and remuneration into the process
5 Learning sets and cross-functional teams with validation of materials and accreditation of individual's learning by an appropriate academic institution
6 Two-way communication between your own company and other global brand leaders to maximize learning

Steps in development

Experience of running EI programmes has led me to the conclusion that inviting people to carry out further development tasks after training is challenging. Even the most careful contracting in the world is challenged by people's return to work. I suggest a more lateral approach:

● Improve the work environment to make learning a part of your business as usual.
● Make doing development activities a way of preparing for, conducting and reflecting on routine events at work.

Use the EI development exercises contained in this book to prepare, conduct and reflect on everyday events. The concept is that your way of 'being' will be different, rather than the way you use techniques driven by your task-orientation. Plan to run exercises utilizing as many relationships as possible seeking collaboration with others and using the book to set the context if others are anxious or confused.

Emotions are not merely the remnant of our pre-sapient past but rather they form important characteristics of an active, searching and thinking human being. Anything that is a novelty, a discrepancy or an interruption generates a visceral response, while our cognitive system interprets the world as threatening, exciting, frightening or joyful.

The human world is so replete with emotions, not because we are animals at heart, but because it is so full of things that elate or threaten us. With new research into the nature of emotional experience and expression, it is possible to enquire into the role of emotions in adaptive behaviour – your successors may be the result of a new form of natural selection.

If Darwin was right, what will be the process of natural selection for humans in the 21st century? Will emotional intelligence have been a positive selection factor? Selection might be based upon those able to manage the stresses without unbalancing mind and body; the office jungle; commuting and supermarket shopping in the peak period; and other aspects of everyday 21st-century life.

Of those organizations that adapt to survive, which will endure and why?

I hope that you will conclude (as I did) that, once started, developing your EQ becomes a life-long enquiry into the joys and mysteries of being human.

Summary

The chapter has covered steps and techniques within them to design your own programme for intentional change:

- Getting on the right path with a beneficial and closed-loop employee life cycle

- The value of keeping a journal for your Personal Development Plan (PDP)

- How to do a professional analysis

- An analysis of strengths, weaknesses, opportunities and threats to inform your PDP

- An analysis of the skills knowledge and experience required for your current role or future aspirations

- How to prioritize needs

- Exploration of the benefits of the employee life cycle and the consequences of gaps in processes or connections

Questions (answers at the back)

1. **Which of the following reflect the benefits of a closed loop employee life cycle?**
a) There is 100 per cent achievement of objectives and cost base is continually improved ❏
b) Employee capability remains fresh and in line with required company capabilities ❏
c) Feedback loop means that no one is recruited to do an impossible job ❏
d) Morale of staff is low along with productivity – this is transmitted to partner relationships ❏

2. **Which of the following reflect the symptoms of an incomplete employee life cycle?**
a) Early negative attitudes mean that people stay for a redundancy payout ❏
b) Low productivity, high number of accidents and absenteeism occur ❏
c) Low morale of staff leaks to customer relationships ❏
d) Bottom line results are poor and cost base is high ❏

3. **Which one of the following is a correct employee life cycle process?**
a) Recruit and Select ❏
b) Induction and Orientalization ❏
c) 360° Performance Approval ❏
d) Continuous Professional Definition ❏

4. **Which of the following are not recorded by a learning log questionnaire?**
a) Learning goals being worked on ❏
b) Record of the last exercise completed ❏
c) What learning occurred ❏
d) Your manager's criticism during the exercise ❏

5. **Which of the following are headings in your EI exercise log?**
a) Exercise number ❏
b) Date completed ❏
c) With whom ❏
d) Learning highlights ❏

6. **Which of the following reflect advice on setting up a Personal Development Plan?**
a) A PDP should start with a baseline entry developed using some techniques, e.g. professional development analysis ❏
b) The PDP should be maintained throughout training. If possible, it can be updated every day using the learning outcomes, session objectives or teaching points as a structure ❏
c) Personal development progress should be judged against agreed criteria for every job ❏
d) Any gaps identified can be developed through a variety of methods, such as coaching and formal learning events ❏

Surviving in tough times

During tough times, you need a keen edge to get ahead of competitors, whether for a job, a contract or a university place. Research that showed that up to 90 per cent of personal performance effectiveness was due to emotional savvy more than technical knowhow (though both are essential) rocked the business community. It's good news that unlike IQ (which plateaus at about 11 years of age) emotional intelligence can be improved by self-study at any age. Practise what you read and you'll maximize your chances of winning.

Here are ten crucial tips that you can use to make sure you stand out from the crowd.

1 Make a date with your inner self

As opposed to being in the 'here and now', alert and engaged at work, how much time do we spend in our own head mulling over disappointments or in the world of fantasy?

It's said that when the going gets tough, the tough get going. However, being tough doesn't mean you need to be ruthless or out of tune with the impact you have on people, or insensitive to the emotional states of others. The fundamental building block of higher EQ is self-awareness; it's the root and branch of being resilient, bouncing back from setbacks and becoming stronger through adverse times.

2 Find your inner leader

Quite often, renowned great leaders are teased or derided in the press, yet they receive outstanding loyalty from their staff. You have to ask yourself what extraordinary qualities have earned them that loyalty. Sometimes it's not just about how they treat staff face to face; it's about the kind of freedoms they allow that empower people, and which, despite an adverse climate, in turn engender loyalty. Answer these questions: am I going to be the good leader I hoped I would be? Can I cope with the pressure? Learning to heighten your self-awareness will contribute powerfully to greater success and raise your motivation.

3 Master your good habits

> *Man's life work is a master piece or a shame*
> *as each little habit has been perfectly or*
> *carelessly formed.*
>
> Joltn Ruskin

Does any child start something intending it to become a bad habit? In finding entertainment in doing something or in pleasing an authority figure, we identify the behaviour as advantageous; thus, it becomes habitual. It's no surprise that breaking bad habits is harder than acquiring them. However, by understanding our brain functioning and instincts, we can learn to sustain the job or contract by demonstrating the behaviours the employer finds productive and worth paying for.

4 Make a stress management contract with yourself

List what you need to start, stop, do less of and do more of in order to relax. Identify sources of stress and beneficial management strategies. Few people are likely to argue that the last decade has been challenging for many of us across the planet. Therefore, the ability to cope in a sustainable way with externally induced stress is useful. Learning how to identify and eliminate internally-focussed stress from inappropriate responses to perceived threats is vital to long-term health, both physiological and mental.

5 Get fit for change

Change has been forced on every organization in the last decade regardless of sector so upgrading your managerial skills to cope with change and to engender change readiness in others is essential. Creating an EI culture can be part of learning to renew and reinvent your organization and it will help diagnose and explore change to create change readiness.

6 Create an innovative, emotionally-literate culture

You have to be *the change you wish for the world.*

Gandhi

To succeed in today's global economy we probably need to move from the knowledge economy to an 'ideas economy' where the whole brain's capacity is utilized to create innovations and to make them robust. Taking a leading role in transforming the organization, you'll need to coach others and to take them with you. Learning how to generate an EI programme helps to take advantage of being a learning organization in which ideas, insight and innovation are nurtured in a trusting climate at work.

7 Master self-directed learning to get an edge

Take charge of your personal development: start the good habit of Personal Development Planning (PDP) and monitoring your own performance.

Identify discriminating competencies that separate superior performers from average performers and include them in your plan. Identify core competencies – i.e. characteristics that people would have in common for a role needed to get the basic job done. Last year's superior performance will now form the core competency of the team.

Taking charge of your PDP demonstrates aspiration, commitment and a drive to succeed.

8 Improve your employability prospects

It can be very daunting joining the workplace after university and being put into a management stream, finding yourself leading people when you are only a couple of years beyond your teenage years. Employers' feedback says that people are coming to them from education without skills in team working, flair in communication, work ethics and commitment to their employer. Developing your EI will demonstrate your commitment to these capabilities to get you ahead of competitors.

9 Practise increasing your resilience

In this climate, you need to have stamina, be able to control your impulses and emotional reactions, generate optimism appropriately, be empathic with others and be self-directed.

10 Engender trust in others

Once trust is breached, even the hero becomes a heretic; so your good intentions are disbelieved. Stagnating organizations have little trust in teams and between managers. A lot of money can be wasted as a result. To gain competitive advantage with rivals, you need to be able to share ideas and gain credit appropriately. Good managers increase trust, generating the teams' ability to work under increasing pressure, thus creating a better future through the initiative of individuals shared between members of your team.

Answers

Sunday: 1c; 2b; 3d; 4c; 5d; 6b.

Monday: 1c; 2b; 3d; 4c; 5b.

Tuesday: 1b; 2a; 3b; 4a; 5a.

Wednesday: 1d; 2a; 3c; 4d; 5d.

Thursday: 1d; 2b; 3b; 4d; 5 all; 6a,b,c; 7b.

Friday: 1a,d; 2b,d; 3a; 4c; 5 d.

Saturday: 1a,b,c; 2b,c,d; 3a; 4d; 5d; 6 all.